Why?

Experiments
for the
Young Scientist

Dave Prochnow and
Kathy Prochnow

Chelsea House Publishers

Philadelphia

Disclaimer

This book deals with subjects, materials, and procedures that can be hazardous to your health. Use extreme caution when performing this book's experiments. Do not attempt to perform any of these experiments unless you fully comprehend all of the materials' associated handling precautions. If you lack this information, consult with a science teacher or another adult.

Although every possible safeguard has been employed in ensuring the accuracy of this book's information, neither the authors nor Chelsea House Publishers can be held liable for damages or injuries that could result from the application, misinterpretation, and/or misapplication of the materials and procedures that are discussed in this book.

This Chelsea House Edition with Permission of the McGraw-Hill Companies.

Product or brand names used in this book may be trade names or trademarks. Where we believe that there may be proprietary claims to such trade names or trademarks, the name has been used with an initial capital or it has been capitalized in the style used by the name claimant. Regardless of the capitalization used, all such names have been used in an editorial manner without any intent to convey endorsement of or other affiliation with the name claimant. Neither the author nor the publisher intends to express any judgment as to the validity or legal status of any such proprietary claims.

Library of Congress Cataloging-in-Publication Data

Prochnow, Dave.
    Why? : experiments for the young scientist /
Dave Prochnow and Kathy Prochnow.
    p. cm.
    Originally published: Blue Ridge Summit, Pa.: Tab Books, c 1993.
    Includes bibliographical references and index.
    Summary: Presents forty-nine experiments for the young engineer, astronomer, chemist, meteorologist, biologist, and physicist.
    ISBN 0-7910-4849-7 (hardcover)
    1. Science—Experiments—Juvenile literature. 2. Engineering-Experiments—Juvenile literature. [1. Science—Experiments. 2. Experiments.] I. Prochnow, Kathy. II. Title.
Q164.P85 1997
507'.8—dc21   97-26989
                                        CIP
                                        AC

Contents

Introduction

You are about to take a journey into the world of science. This encounter will be unlike any that you have ever had. You won't have to take any tests or quizzes, or learn any complex formulas. And it is impossible to make a mistake.

Your excursion begins as a young scientist: engineer, astronomer, chemist, meteorologist, biologist, and physicist. And like the scientist, you will explore the world of questions by performing experiments, making observations, and recording results. A few of the scientific areas you will explore include:

structural engineering
architecture
computer science
botany
entomology
ecology
electronics
geology
paleontology
astronomy
chemistry
mathematics
meteorology
physics

How to Use This Book The book is divided into six parts: The Young Engineer, The Young Astronomer, The Young Chemist, The Young Meteorologist, The Young Biologist, and The Young Physicist. In each part, you will find a series of hands-on experiments that answer complicated questions in science. Questions like: "Why does soap make suds?" "Why does iron rust?" and "Why do helium balloons rise?"

Each experiment is a self-contained study; therefore, you can perform any experiment at any time. You needn't read the chapters in order nor do every experiment. We suggest that you begin with the subjects that interest you most and that you work with an adult who enjoys exploring the scientific world as much as you do.

When you look at the experiments, you'll notice that each has five sections:

Why? Each experiment begins with a *why* question. The question is the reason for conducting the experiment.

Materials This is a list of the tools and supplies that you will need to perform the experiment.

Procedure Written as step-by-step directions, this section tells you how to do the experiment.

Results This is a brief description of the expected reactions, conclusions, and results of the experiment.

Further studies This section has more information—and sometimes more experiments—for a better understanding of the *why* question.

In the laboratory, good scientists keep good records of all their experiments. And so should you. As you do each experiment, write down three things: what you did, what you saw, and what you think happened. These are your procedures, observations, and conclusions. A good place for your records is a wire-bound notebook.

Before starting any experiment in this book, be sure you and an adult—your parent or teacher—read the experiment together. Some of the experiments call for using scissors, a hot iron, burning candles, harsh chemicals, and other dangerous materials. Learn how to use these materials safely.

Another thing to do before starting an experiment: Discuss with your parents or teachers whether you can do the experiment independently or if you must have assistance. Your parents or teachers may prefer that you do all the experiments with them.

The following symbols are used throughout the book as a guide to what you might be able to do independently and what you should do with adult supervision.

Materials or tools used in this experiment could be dangerous. Work with an adult and learn how to handle sharp tools or combustible or toxic materials and how to protect surfaces.

 Wear protective gloves that are flame retardant and heat resistant. Handling hot objects can burn your hands. Protect surfaces beneath hot materials—do not set pots of boiling water or very hot objects directly on tabletops or counters. Use towels or heat pads.

 Wear protective safety goggles to safeguard your eyes from shattering glass or other hazards that could damage your eyes.

 Burning candles, canned heat, or another source of flame is used in this experiment. Work with an adult. Do not wear loose clothing. Tie your hair back. When handling candles, wear protective gloves—hot wax can burn. Never leave a flame unattended. Extinguish flame properly. Protect surfaces beneath burning candles.

 The stove, oven, boiling water, or other hot materials are used in this experiment. Work with an adult. Keep other small children away from boiling water and burners.

 Electricity is used in this experiment. Work with an adult. Plug appliances in carefully. Turn appliance on according to instructions.

 Plants and leaves are used in this experiment. Ask an adult to identify the poisonous ones—poison ivy, poison oak, and poison sumac—that you should not pick. Do not taste any leaves. The leaves of many plants are safe to touch but not safe to taste.

 Chemicals, fertilizers, soap, plants, leaves, moldy bread, or moldy fruits are used in this experiment. Do not taste—or eat—these materials. They can burn your mouth or make you very sick.

Disclaimer

Although every possible safeguard has been employed in ensuring the accuracy of this book's information, neither the authors nor TAB Books can be held liable for damages or injuries that could result from the application, misinterpretation, and/or misapplication of the materials and procedures that are discussed in this book.

Part I
The Young Engineer

Successfully combining art and science is the foundation of engineering. An understanding of art is important to the engineer as he or she tries to make a product that is visually pleasing. The science of engineering ensures that the engineer's product will work.

For example, the engineer who designs a bridge must make sure that the bridge functions as a bridge. Then the engineer must determine if the design is compatible with the surrounding environment. In other words, the bridge must work and it must blend in with the "look and feel" of its location. Balancing those science and art requirements is the base of engineering.

Why do helium balloons rise?

Materials
- ❏ Several balloons
- ❏ Can of *helium* (available in florist shops)

Procedure

1. Carefully inflate one balloon with helium. Seal the balloon by tying the end in a knot.
2. Inflate another balloon with air. (You can simply blow this one up.) Seal the balloon by tying the end in a knot.
3. Hold the helium-filled balloon in your right hand and the air-filled balloon in your left hand.
4. Release both balloons at the same time.
5. Observe the results.

Results   Helium is a chemical element. The chemical symbol for helium is He. Helium is an extremely lightweight, colorless gas. Only hydrogen gas weighs less than helium. Because of its lightness, a helium-filled balloon will rise. A hydrogen-filled balloon will also rise. Unfortunately, hydrogen gas is extremely dangerous, and it will explode violently when it makes contact with a spark or flame. Therefore, safe lighter-than-air airship travel uses helium gas. *Sir William Ramsay* discovered helium in 1895.

Further studies   Now that you understand that helium is lighter than air, see how much weight the helium balloon can carry as a payload. Attach small objects such as paper clips or pieces of masking tape to the balloon. Release the balloon and observe the results. What is the maximum weight that a helium-filled balloon can lift?

By the way, why does the air-filled balloon fall to the ground when it is released? If it is filled with air, shouldn't it remain in the same position that you released it in?

For fun, see if you can find the balloon without a match in FIG. 1-1.

Did you know?

○ The first balloon flight in the United States took place in Philadelphia on January 9, 1793.

○ The first transatlantic balloon flight took place in 1978. Balloonists, flying the helium-filled Double Eagle II, set distance (3108 miles) and endurance records (137 hours 6 minutes).

1-1 Which balloon is different?

Experiment 2

Why do pilots wear parachutes?

Materials
- ❐ 3-inch piece of string
- ❐ AA battery
- ❐ Cellophane (clear) tape
- ❐ 11-inch square handkerchief (or piece of old sheet)
- ❐ Four 8-inch pieces of string

Procedure
1. Wrap two complete turns of the 3-inch string around the battery.
2. Hold this string in place with a piece of the tape. Set the prepared battery aside for a moment.
3. Lay the handkerchief flat on a table.
4. Tie one 8-inch piece of string to each of its four corners.
5. Bring all four of the loose ends of the string pieces together and tie them in a knot.
6. Tie the loose string end from the battery to the knot formed by the handkerchief string pieces.
7. Your parachute is now ready for testing.
8. Drop the parachute and watch what happens.

Results
When the parachute opens, air resistance increases underneath the handkerchief. This air resistance slows the speed of the parachute's *descent*, or fall. Using a standard parachute, an average-sized pilot slows his descent enough that his final landing speed is roughly equal to jumping from a 10-foot-high platform.

Further studies
To learn more about how parachutes work, make several parachutes, each time modifying your design a little. First, change the size. You might try using a 7-inch square; then a 14-inch square for the parachute's *canopy*, or top. After tying the battery to each parachute, drop each one and observe the results.

Next, try cutting a small hole in the top of the canopy. Drop the parachute again and watch the results. Finally, put four sticks under the canopy, and try to make a pyramid-shaped parachute similar to da Vinci's. Of all the parachutes, which is best at slowing the speed of descent?

For more information about parachutes, look in an encyclopedia or read *Parachutes: How They Work* by Eloise Engle.

Did you know? ○ Jean Pierre Blanchard, a French aeronaut, used the first parachute to drop a dog from a balloon in 1785.

○ *Leonardo da Vinci* is generally credited with being the inventor of the parachute. His original design, created in 1495, was called a "tent roof." (See FIG. 2-1.) This pyramid-shaped parachute is very different from the design used by today's pilots.

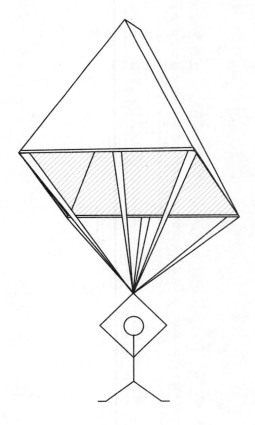

2-1 Leonardo da Vinci's "tent-roof" parachute design

Why are paper airplanes so aerobatic?

Materials ❏ Several sheets of 8½-x-11-inch paper

Procedure 1. Fold the paper as shown on the airplane plan in FIG. 3-1: (1.) Fold paper in half along the dotted line. (2.) Fold the corners down at the dotted line. (3.) Fold the edges down along the dotted lines. (4.) Fold down again along the dotted lines. Your airplane is now ready for flying.

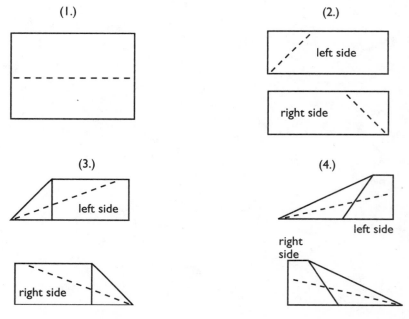

3-1 How to make a paper airplane

2. Fly your airplane.

3. Add elevators and *ailerons* to your plane by making the folds shown in FIG. 3-2. Fold up along the dotted line. (You can fold the elevators and ailerons down, and the airplane will behave differently.)

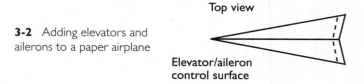

3-2 Adding elevators and ailerons to a paper airplane

Top view

Elevator/aileron control surface

4. Fly your airplane and observe the changes.

5. Add rudder control to your airplane by making the fold shown in FIG. 3-3. Fold along the dotted line to make a rudder.

6. Fly your airplane and observe the new changes.

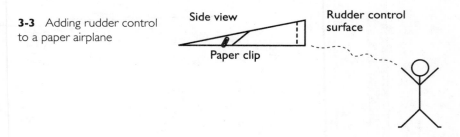

3-3 Adding rudder control to a paper airplane

Side view

Rudder control surface

Paper clip

7. Add weight and balance to your airplane with a paper clip. (See FIG. 3-3.)

8. Again, make several flights with the changes on the airplane.

Results A good paper airplane design exhibits control over four forces: *lift, thrust, drag,* and *gravity.* Separate features of the airplane design deal with each of these forces.

The airplane's lift comes from the shape of the wings. Wings with a more curved top surface and a flatter bottom surface will generate greater lift.

Thrust is produced by tossing the paper airplane into the air with your hand. The harder the toss, the greater the thrust.

As the air moves over the airplane's wings and around its fuselage, friction is created. This friction is the drag on the airplane.

Finally, the total weight of the airplane is affected by gravity. In order for level flight at a steady speed to occur, lift must be equal to gravity and thrust must be equal to drag.

Control surfaces are used for altering an airplane's position during flight. The three flight controls are *rudder, elevators,* and *ailerons.* (See FIG. 3-4.) Briefly, the rudder makes the airplane move from side to side (yaw), the elevators move the airplane up and down (pitch), and the ailerons cause either the left or the right wing to dip (roll). Your paper airplane design combines the elevator and aileron functions for *aerobatic* flight. Aerobatics are the controlled maneuvers of an airplane in flight.

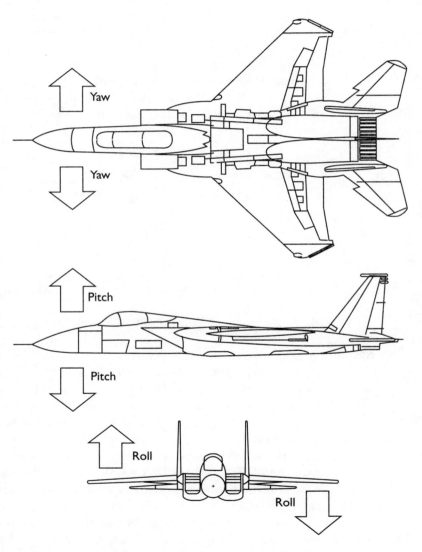

3-4 How a rudder, elevators, and ailerons affect a plane's position

Try flying other paper airplane designs. (See FIGS. 3-5 and 3-6.) For the ring-design plane in FIG. 3-5: (1.) Cut two strips from a sheet of paper. (2.) Form a ring with each strip and tape each strip's ends together. (3.) Attach each ring to a straw. (4.) This airplane follows a gentle flight path. You can vary the ring size and placement for controlling the airplane.

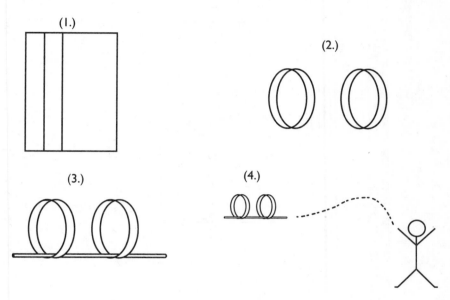

(1.)

(2.)

(3.)

(4.)

3-5 A unique ring-design paper airplane

To make the space-age Star Cruiser in FIG. 3-6: (1.) Fold paper in half lengthwise (dotted line *A*); open out flat. Matching points *S* and *R*, fold along dotted line *B*. Open out flat. Fold along dotted line *C*. Open out flat.

(2.) Bring point *X* over to point *Y*. At the same time, bring corner *V* over to corner *W*. (Your plane should now look like step 3.)

(3.) Along dotted line *D*, fold the top layer back to the right. Bring point *P* down. (Plane should look like step 4.)

(4.) Fold the whole plane in half along dotted line A. (5.) For the tail section, push point *R* up through the middle along dotted line *E*. (6.) Fold the wing sections 1 and 2 along dotted line *G*.

Observe the way the two planes fly; then change their control surfaces for aerobatics. Again, watch the way they fly. Is one design more adept at a particular maneuver than another? By using all of these flight experiences, try designing your own paper airplane that can perform a perfect loop. (See FIG. 3-7.)

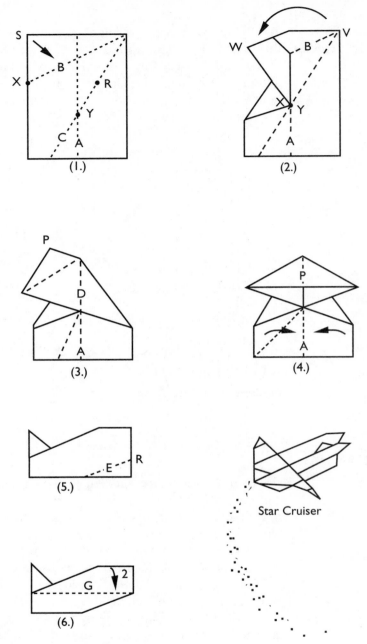

3-6 A space-age Star Cruiser paper airplane

Figure 3-8 shows two other airplane aerobatic maneuvers that are often used by planes in air shows. Which control surfaces must the pilot use to perform the maneuvers? Continue experimenting with the control surfaces to make your airplane perform stunts.

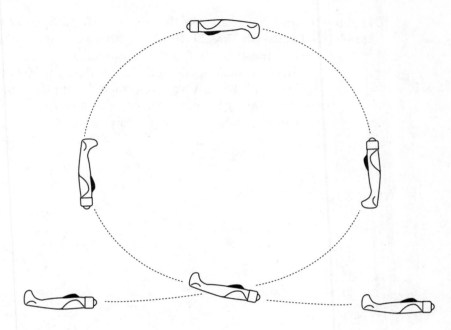

3-7 A loop

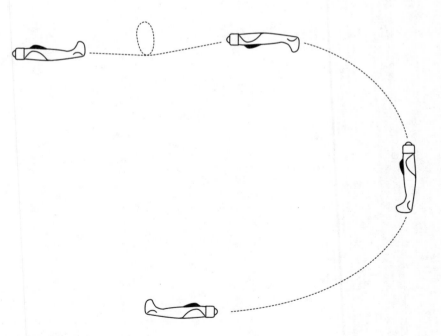

3-8 An Immelmann turn

○ Amelia Earhart was the first woman to fly solo across the Atlantic Ocean on May 20, 1932 (exactly five years after the same feat was accomplished by Charles Lindbergh).

○ The first rocket-powered aircraft flew for 50 seconds on June 30, 1939. This aircraft was a German design known as the Heinkel HE 176. The first United States rocket-powered aircraft, the Avion/ Northrop MX-324, flew on July 5, 1944.

Why is the brain called the "world's greatest computer"?

Materials ❏ Yourself

Procedure 1. Answer the following questions without using any paper for calculating.

8 × 5=
32 + 15=
521 − 301=
72 ÷ 12=

2. Now answer these questions:

How many sides does the Pentagon Building in Washington, D.C.
have?
How many feet are in 1 mile?
What colors are in France's national flag?

Results Did you answer each question? How did you arrive at your answers?
The ability to answer such questions underlines the computing
power of the human brain. It would be impossible for any computer
to answer a variety of questions without using an elaborate program.
Yet the human brain is able to answer hundreds of questions without depending on any outside programming. Furthermore, the human brain is able to make judgments based on personal experiences.
For example, to plan a trip from your hometown to Yellowstone
National Park in Wyoming, you must organizing hundreds of different

thoughts. A computer, even with thorough programming, would have a hard time developing all the requirements that are needed for organizing such a trip. In fact, a computer can't think. It can only do what you tell it to do. This limitation in computers is rapidly changing, however. Some computers are now using a programming language that gives them an artificial ability to think. This ability to think in computers is called artificial intelligence or AI.

Further studies Try teaching a younger child to tie his or her shoes. If you can, work with a very young child—the younger, the better.

When teaching the very young, you must break the task into many small steps and do only one step at a time. It's the same with programming a computer. Everything must be done in a simple step-by-step fashion. In this way, you can equate the task of teaching the very young to the task of programming a computer.

Did you know?
○ About 100 years ago, Johann Dase, a German, performed the mathematical feat of multiplying 79,532,853 by 93,758,479 in just 54 seconds. His computer was nature's best—his brain.
○ Your brain has roughly 14 billion cells and can send messages to any part of your body with amazing speed—around 250 miles an hour.

Experiment 5

Why are computers good with math?

Materials
- ☐ Heavy paper (4 × 12 inches)
- ☐ Ruler
- ☐ Scissors
- ☐ Cellophane (clear) tape
- ☐ Pen

Procedure
1. Cut two strips of heavy paper. One is 1 × 12 inches and the other is 2 × 12 inches.
2. Cut two 1-inch squares from the remaining heavy paper.
3. Fold down ¼-inch sides along the length of the larger strip. Open flat.
4. Lay the smaller strip inside the larger strip and fold the larger strip's sides over the smaller strip.
5. Place a 1-inch square on each end of the strips.
6. Tape the 1-inch squares in place along the folded sides of the larger strip. Be sure to leave the remaining sides free so that the smaller strip can slide back and forth lengthwise.
7. Center the smaller strip inside the larger strip.
8. Use the pen to mark ½-inch intervals on one of the long sides of the larger strip. Duplicate these marks on the center of the smaller strip.
9. Number the interval marks with whole numbers starting with 0.
10. Your paper computer (also called a slide rule) is now ready for addition and subtraction problems. (See FIG. 5-1.)

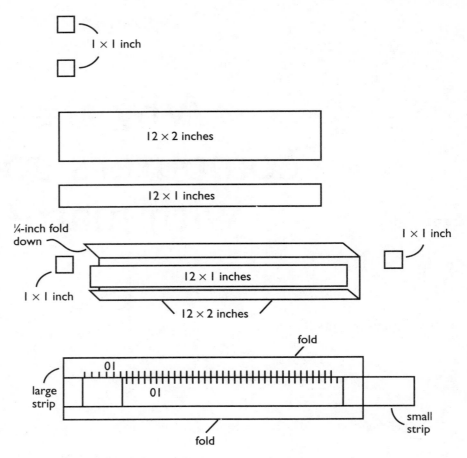

5-1 A simple addition/subtraction paper computer

Results This *analog* computer measures the length of the two pieces of paper and gives the final length as either a sum or a difference. Using this paper computer is similar to operating a slide rule. The 0 on the smaller strip serves as the index mark during both addition and subtraction problem solving. In addition, the 0 is placed opposite the first factor in the equation to be solved. The sum can then be read from the larger strip opposite the second factor on the smaller strip. For example:

To find the answer to 15 + 7:

1. Slide the smaller strip until the 0 lines up with 15 on the larger strip.
2. Locate 7 on the smaller strip.
3. Read the number on the larger strip that is opposite 7.
4. This is the answer.

Subtraction is just the opposite of addition. In subtraction, the 0 on the smaller strip is used for reading the answer from the larger strip. For example:

To find the answer to 13 − 6:

1. Slide the smaller strip until 6 is lined up with 13 on the larger strip.
2. Locate 0 on the smaller strip.
3. Read the number on the larger strip that is opposite the 0.
4. This is the answer.

Further studies If you square a number—multiply a number by itself—it forms a square. Try it. Multiply 2 × 2. The answer is 4. Now arrange 4 pennies in a square pattern. What do you have? Two pennies on each side or 2 × 2. Practice with 3 × 3 and 4 × 4.

Did you know? ○ The product, or answer, of 9 times any number from 1 to 10 adds up to 9. For example:

9 × 2 = 18; 1 + 8 = 9.
9 × 3 = 27; 2 + 7 = 9.
9 × 8 = 72; 7 + 2 = 9.
6 × 9 = 54; 5 + 4 = 9.

Experiment 6

Why do bicyclists wear helmets?

Materials
- ❏ Serrated knife
- ❏ 6-inch Styrofoam ball
- ❏ Grapefruit spoon or teaspoon
- ❏ Egg
- ❏ Two rubber bands

Procedure

1. Using the knife, very carefully cut the Styrofoam ball in half. Place the ball on a breadboard or other cutting surface when you cut. And be sure to cut toward the board and not toward your body or hand.
2. With the grapefruit spoon, scoop out the center of each Styrofoam half. The hole should be large enough to hold the egg. Leave the walls of the Styrofoam ball as thick as possible.
3. Put the egg inside the ball and hold the ball closed with the rubber bands.
4. Test the Styrofoam holder's ability to protect the egg by dropping the holder and egg from a height of 10 feet.
5. Open the holder. Did the egg's shell break?

Results The Styrofoam holder protected the egg inside by absorbing the energy of the fall and the impact. In a similar way, a bicyclist's helmet protects the bicyclist's head in a fall. The sturdy, lightweight molded foam in the helmet absorbs the energy of an impact.

Further studies Now that you know why helmets are important to bicyclists, let's look at cars and their bumpers. Basically, bumpers are for absorbing the impact of a low-speed accident. Well-designed, impact-absorbing bumpers can reduce damage to the rest of the car.

Car makers manufacture impact-absorbing bumpers in two ways: (1) The bumper is mounted on a spring or shock absorber. This flexible mount helps reduce the impact to an automobile during slow-speed accidents of less than 5 miles an hour. (2) The bumper is especially designed to collapse as it absorbs the impact. This form of protection is used for moderate speed accidents between 5 and 25 miles per hour.

Other parts of the car also use the collapse-on-impact design to protect people in the passenger compartment. For example, the hood of the car crumples, the steering wheel breaks away, and the windshield pulverizes.

Try making your own impact-absorbing bumper for a toy car. Cut a "bumper" from an old foam rubber carpet pad. Cover the bumper with a smooth piece of aluminum foil, trying not to wrinkle the foil as you work. Tape the bumper to the car.

Now, your car is ready for a minor fender-bender. Have your car collide slowly with another toy car. The foil fender will show creases from the collision, but the foam rubber should help reform the bumper.

Did you know?

○ Modern Indianapolis 500 racing cars are designed with impact absorbing construction so that a driver can avoid serious injury even in a 200-mile-per-hour crash.

○ The ends of guide rails on some highways have large blocks of Styrofoam-type material in front of them to absorb energy if a vehicle strikes them.

Why does soil erosion occur?

Materials
- ❏ Two 8-x-10-x-½-inch plywood boards
- ❏ Potting soil
- ❏ 8-x-10-inch piece of sod
- ❏ Water hose with sprinkling head

Procedure
1. Work on this experiment outside. Place a layer of potting soil on one of the plywood boards. Spread the soil 2 inches deep over the entire board.
2. Place the sod on the other plywood board.
3. Raise one end of each board 4 inches above a flat surface.
4. Turn on the water hose. Adjust the sprinkler head for a fine mist.
5. Direct the water from the hose at the board containing the potting soil. Hold the water on the board for 3 minutes.
6. Stop watering the potting soil.
7. Direct the water at the board holding the sod. Run the water over the sod for 3 minutes.

Results Soil that lacks ground cover is subject to *erosion*, the washing away of soil. The result of erosion is ground that lacks high-quality topsoil. Additionally, the eroded soil becomes deeply marked with *gullies* and washed out areas. On the other hand, soil that is protected by ground cover, grass, and trees is less likely to erode.

Ground cover, grass, and trees prevent erosion in two ways: First, grass and trees reduce the impact of the water drops hitting the soil surface. Therefore, the water strikes the soil with less force. Second, the root system of grass and trees holds the soil and absorbs the water that soaks into the ground.

Another method for reducing soil erosion is contour plowing. Contour plowing moves the soil into small ridges that run perpendicular to the natural flow of water. These ridges then catch and hold the water so it doesn't run along the ground and wash away the top soil.

Further studies
Spread the two plywood boards with a 2-inch layer of potting soil. This time use contour plowing and a ground cover to prevent erosion. On one board, which you can label contour plowing, use your finger to dig parallel furrows that are perpendicular to the tilt of the raised board. On the other board, plant grass seed on the potting soil.

To plant the grass, sprinkle the seeds on the soil. Keep them moist with water. In several days, you should notice that some grass is sprouting.

When the grass is fairly thick and strong, test the erosion prevention of each board. Did the water erode the soil? Which method prevented erosion the longest? Can you think of other methods for preventing erosion?

Did you know?
○ The word "erosion" comes from the Latin term for "gnaw away."
○ On a huge scale, the Grand Canyon of the Colorado River is an example of erosion by water.

Experiment 8

Why doesn't an arch fall down?

Materials
- ❑ 8½-x-11-inch piece of thin paper
- ❑ 8½-x-11-inch piece of thin cardboard
- ❑ One sheet of 2-x-36-x-36-inch Styrofoam
- ❑ Serrated knife
- ❑ Nontoxic white glue or masking tape

Procedure

1. Trace the arch *templates* onto the thin paper and cut them out. (See FIG. 8-1.)
2. Use the cutout templates to make sturdier patterns from the cardboard.
3. Ask an adult to help you with this step. Using the knife and the cardboard patterns, carefully cut blocks from the Styrofoam. You'll need 2 *springer* blocks, 1 *keystone* block, and 10 *voussoir* blocks.
4. Glue or tape the blocks together to form a semicircular arch. (See FIGS. 8-2 and 8-3.)

Results An arch is a weight-bearing opening in which wedge-shaped blocks are joined to form a curved arch. Because of gravity, the arch pushes its sides outward. This outward movement is called thrust.

Thrust is offset by two *buttresses* made from large blocks of masonry. This masonry or brickwork is placed along the side of the arch.

The arch, itself, is made with the specially shaped blocks shown in FIG. 8-2. The arch begins at the springers or skewbacks, which rest on top of the buttresses. Most of the arch consists of voussoirs. These are the wedged-shaped stones that ring the top of the arch. The keystone is the center block in the arch.

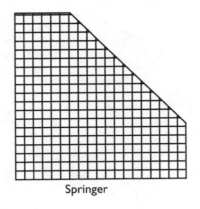

Springer

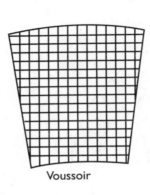

Voussoir

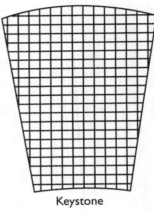

Keystone

8-1 Arch templates

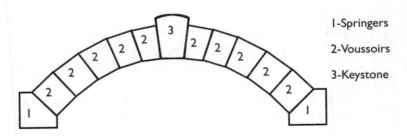

1-Springers

2-Voussoirs

3-Keystone

8-2 Parts of an arch

Various terms describe the dimensions of an arch. The highest point on the arch is called the crown. The width between the arch's springers is the span, and the arch's height from the springers to the keystone is called the rise. What are the measurements of your arch?

Why doesn't an arch fall down?   23

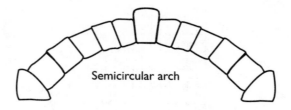

Semicircular arch

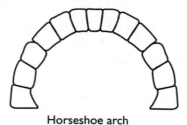

8-3 Types of arches

Horseshoe arch

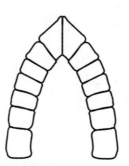

Lancet arch

Further studies The arch that you built is called a semicircular arch. This is the simplest arch form. Other arch shapes include the horseshoe arch and the lancet arch. (See FIG. 8-3). Based on the illustration of these two arch shapes, can you build an example of each?

Did you know?
○ The ancient Romans built arches of wood and stone to serve as bridges. The An-Chi Bridge, an arch bridge built by the Chinese in about 600 A.D., is still in use today.
○ Modern arch bridges are made of steel and can carry cars and trains. The Sydney Harbour Bridge in Australia stretches nearly 4 miles.

Part 2
The Young Astronomer

Astronomy is one of the oldest sciences. Early human beings frequently looked to the night sky for guidance in their everyday lives. This daily dependence on the activities of the sky slowly gave rise to the scientific study of both the sky and the motions of its objects. The objects that are found in the sky cover a wide range of topics; there are planets, stars, *comets,* meteors, and asteroids. A collective name for these objects is heavenly bodies. The study of the heavenly bodies forms the basis of astronomy.

Experiment 9

Why do shadows form during the day?

Materials   ❑ Three rounded toothpicks
❑ 6-inch Styrofoam ball
❑ Flashlight

Procedure 1. Push one toothpick halfway into the ball. This toothpick will represent the North Pole of the earth.
2. Exactly opposite the toothpick, push another toothpick halfway into the ball. This toothpick will represent the South Pole.
3. Now anywhere between the two poles, push a third toothpick halfway into the ball.
4. Turn on the flashlight, turn out all other lights in the room, and aim the light at the ball. The flashlight will represent the sun.
5. Tilt the ball so the North Pole is pointed slightly toward the light.
6. Slowly rotate the earth on its *axis* (the toothpicks) without moving the sun.
7. Observe the formation of shadows on the earth. (See FIG. 9-1.)

Results   As the earth rotates, or spins, the sun appears to rise and fall each day. This rotation is actually movement of the earth around an imaginary line formed by the two poles. Another name for this line is the earth's axis.

The earth completes a rotation on its axis once every 23 hours, 56 minutes, and 4.1 seconds. Scientists approximate this value as 24 hours. Therefore, one day or one complete rotation on earth takes 24 hours. The earth rotates toward the east. This movement makes the sun appear to rise in the east each morning and set in the west each evening.

Earth's orbit

Light

from

flashlight

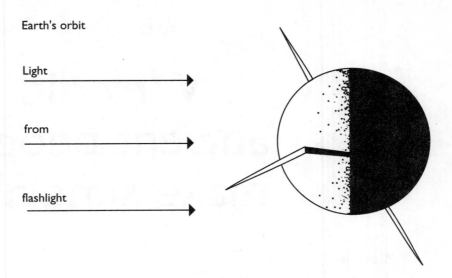

9-1 Shadows forming on the earth

Further studies Place a 6-inch-high object in a window that receives light all day. Record—in a notebook—the date and time, and the height and location of the shadow. Observe the shadow at the same time of day for a couple of months, being certain to record your findings.

As the earth changes its relative location on its axis (precesses) the shadow of the object will move.

Did you know?
○ Our sun completes an orbit around the Milky Way every 225 million years.
○ Our earth is tiny compared to the sun that warms us. One hundred earths could fit around the sun's diameter.

Why did ancient people make sundials?

Materials
- ❏ Compass
- ❏ Heavy cardboard
- ❏ Scissors
- ❏ Protractor
- ❏ Nontoxic white glue

Procedure

1. Using the compass, draw a circle with a 7-inch diameter on the cardboard (FIG. 10-1). Take care when using the compass; its point is extremely sharp.
2. Next, divide the circle in half by drawing a line (diameter) through its center.

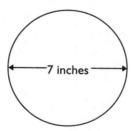 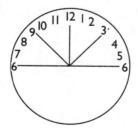

10-1 (Left) Draw a 7-inch-wide circle for the base. (Right) Mark off 12 equal spaces.

3. On half of the circle, mark 12 equal spaces along the arc. Starting at the left and going clockwise, number each mark with these numbers: 6, 7, 8, 9, 10, 11, 12, 1, 2, 3, 4, 5, and 6. The two sixes should be opposite each other and the 12 should be on the mark halfway between them.
4. Next construct the piece that casts the shadow (FIG. 10-2). This triangular piece, called a *gnomon*, has a base that is 3 inches long.

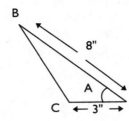

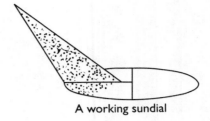

A working sundial

10-2. Making the gnomon.

The other two dimensions are set by the *latitude*, a measurement in degrees from the equator, of your city.

5. To find the latitude of a city near your home, see TABLE 10-1. Use that latitude for angle *A*. With your protractor measure and draw angle *A* at one end of the 3-inch line.

Table 10-1. Sample Latitudes for Your Sundial Gnomon

State	City	Latitude
Alabama	Birmingham	33°
Arizona	Phoenix	34°
Arkansas	Little Rock	35°
California	San Francisco	38°
Colorado	Denver	40°
Connecticut	Hartford	42°
Delaware	Wilmington	40°
Florida	Miami	26°
Georgia	Atlanta	34°
Idaho	Boise	44°
Illinois	Chicago	42°
Indiana	Indianapolis	40°
Iowa	Des Moines	42°
Kansas	Wichita	38°
Kentucky	Louisville	38°
Louisiana	New Orleans	30°
Maine	Portland	44°
Maryland	Baltimore	39°
Massachusetts	Boston	42°
Michigan	Detroit	42°
Minnesota	Minneapolis	45°
Mississippi	Jackson	32°
Missouri	Kansas City	39°
Montana	Billings	48°
Nebraska	Bellevue	41°

continued

Table 10-1. Continued.

State	City	Latitude
Nevada	Reno	40°
New Hampshire	Peterborough	43°
New Jersey	Atlantic City	39°
New Mexico	Albuquerque	35°
New York	New York	41°
North Carolina	Raleigh	36°
North Dakota	Riverdale	48°
Ohio	Cleveland	42°
Oklahoma	Norman	35°
Oregon	Portland	46°
Pennsylvania	Blue Ridge Summit	40°
Rhode Island	Providence	42°
South Carolina	Charleston	33°
South Dakota	Spearfish	44°
Tennessee	Memphis	35°
Texas	Dallas	33°
Utah	Salt Lake City	41°
Vermont	Barre	44°
Virginia	Norfolk	37°
Washington	Seattle	38°
West Virginia	Charleston	38°
Wisconsin	Milwaukee	43°
Wyoming	Laramie	41°

6. Connect *A* to *B* with an 8-inch line.

7. Draw a line from *B* to *C*.

8. Next, glue the gnomon to the circle along its 3-inch side. Point *A* should be near the center of the circle and point *C* should touch mark 12. Place bricks or boxes on either side of the gnomon to hold it in place while the glue sets.

9. If you want, you can place a matching set of numbers on the other half of the circle. These numbers are for night. So, the sundial will not cast a shadow. This step is optional.

10. You can now take your sundial outside on a sunny day to tell the time. When placing your sundial in a location for viewing, make sure that the gnomon is pointed due north. How can you find due north?

Results One early use of the sun's ability to cast changing shadows was the construction of a clock. This clock, also known as a sundial, uses a shadow made by the sun for telling time. How accurate is your sundial clock?

Further studies Just as you used the sun and its shadow to determine time, you can use the sun's shadows to figure out the height of objects. Here's how to figure the height of a tree by using a tape measure, ruler, pencil and paper, and the sun:

With the tape measure, measure the length of the tree's shadow. Stand the ruler next to the tree, and measure the ruler's shadow.

Now you'll need to do a little bit of arithmetic. Multiply the length of the tree's shadow by 12 inches. Divide the result by the length of the ruler's shadow. The answer is the height of the tree.

Did you know?
○ The sundial is probably the oldest device used for measuring time. It was used in Egypt in 2000 BC.
○ Because sundials could only be used during the day, ancient peoples also used water clocks that kept track of time by measuring the flow of water through a bowl-like device and outlet.

Why does the moon appear to change shape?

Materials ❏ Flashlight
❏ 6-inch Styrofoam ball

Procedure 1. Place the flashlight on a shelf (or ask someone to hold the light) directly to the right of your face.
2. Hold the ball at arm's length in front of your face.
3. Turn on the flashlight and turn off all other lights in the room.
4. Slowly rotate your whole body, holding the ball directly in front of you.

Results If you look at the moon every night for a month, you will see that the moon looks different each night. The different shapes that the moon has are called *phases*. These phases happen as the moon *orbits*, or goes around, the earth and reflects sunlight. This movement is a west-to-east direction.

A complete cycle in the moon's phases lasts 29.5 days, about one month. There are six major phase changes that can be seen on the moon: new moon, crescent, first quarter, gibbous, last quarter, and full moon. (See FIGS. 11-1 and 11-2.) At the peak of the moon's phases is the full moon. Each new phase occurs at approximately seven-day intervals. Finally, when the moon is no longer visible, it is known as a new moon.

As the moon is changing from a new moon to a full moon, it is called *waxing*. Conversely, when the moon is changing from a full moon back to a new moon, it is called *waning*.

In this activity, you can see how light reflects off the moon by imagining that you are the earth, the ball is the moon, and the flashlight is the sun. As you face the flashlight, the light reflects off the

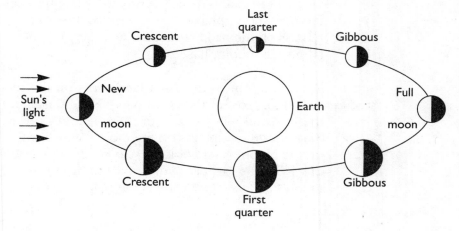

11-1 Moon's orbit around earth

Lunar Orbit Demonstration

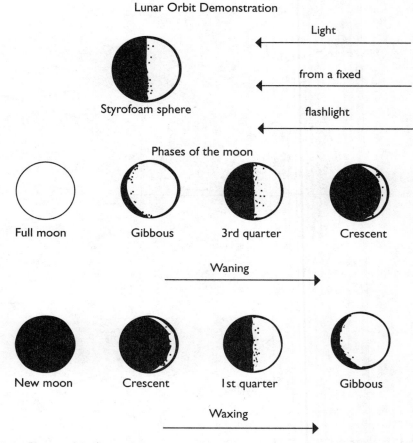

11-2 Phases of the moon

back of the ball in the same way the sunlight reflects off the moon at the new moon phase. When your back is to the flashlight, the light reflects off the ball in the same way the sunlight reflects off the moon at the full moon phase.

Further studies There are numerous visual landmarks on the moon's surface. (See FIG. 11-3). Most of these are only visible during a full moon. During the next full moon, look for these features on the lunar landscape. First, locate mountains on the moon. Which is the highest mountain on the moon? Next, look for seas on the moon. What are the seas of the moon made of? Which is the largest sea? Finally, study the moon's craters. How wide is the biggest crater?

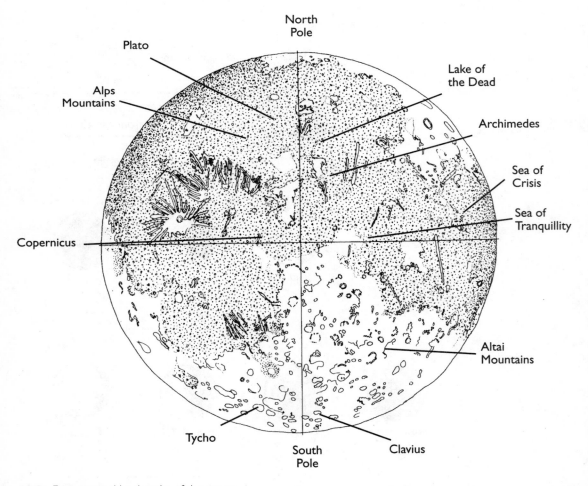

11-3 Features and landmarks of the moon

○ The moon, at 240,000 miles from earth, is our closest natural space neighbor.

○ The moon has no air or water, no wind storms or rain—just extremely hot days and frigid cold nights.

Experiment 12

Why does a solar eclipse block out the sun?

Materials ❏ Flashlight
❏ A large coin such as a quarter

Procedure 1. Place the flashlight on a bookcase (or have someone hold the light) so that the light points directly at the right side of your face.
2. Hold the coin, by its edges, at arm's length directly in front of your face. Turn on the flashlight.
3. Slowly rotate your body until the coin comes between your face and the flashlight. If need be, bring the quarter closer to your face so that it blocks the light from the flashlight.

Results In this activity you have simulated a solar *eclipse*. Here is what happens in a real one:

As the moon passes between the earth and the sun, the moon blocks the sun's light. This is called a solar eclipse. (See FIGS. 12-1 and 12-2.) The solar eclipse moves from the sun's western side to its eastern side. During a total solar eclipse, a small circle of light will leak out around the moon's shadow and form a corona.

A solar eclipse is a predictable event that can only be seen on certain points on the earth. Every 18 years and 11.5 days, a total solar eclipse will cast a shadow 167 miles wide on the earth. The earth's rotation and moon's orbit cause the band of eclipse to move from 1,100 to 5,000 miles per hour across the earth's surface. This speed gives a total solar eclipse a maximum duration of 7 minutes and 40 seconds.

Further studies When the earth comes between the sun and a full moon, a lunar eclipse occurs. Lunar eclipses happen more frequently than solar

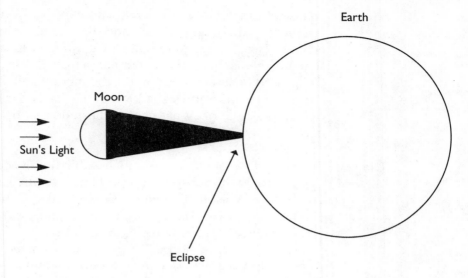

12-1 Solar eclipse

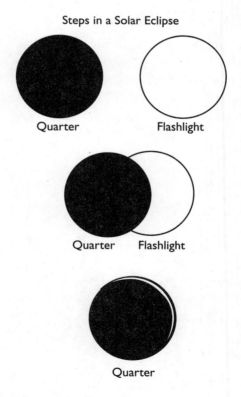

12-2 Sequence of events in a solar eclipse

eclipses. A maximum of three lunar eclipses can be seen during an optimum year. Using a ball and flashlight, demonstrate a lunar eclipse. Two strange phenomena can affect a lunar eclipse. First, a scheduled lunar eclipse may not happen at all. What is the reason for this missed lunar eclipse? Second, the moon might not be completely darkened by the earth's shadow. In this case, the moon might take on a reddish color. What causes the moon to dim to this dull red color?

Did you know?

○ The surface of the sun is unbelievably hot. It seethes and boils at about 6,000°F. Sunspots are cool areas on the sun's surface.

○ Christine Wilson discovered Comet Wilson on August 5, 1986. This comet rivals Halley's Comet in brightness but not in popularity. Whereas Halley's orbits the sun every 76 years and can range as close as 39 million miles from Earth, Comet Wilson has an orbit period of 100 to one million years and travels within 55 million miles of Earth. Comet Wilson came near to Earth on April 30, 1987.

Part 3
The Young
Chemist

The science of chemistry studies the structure and properties of substances and the ways that substances change. All of these areas are related to each other. When a chemical reaction takes place, changes occur in substances. During this process, heat, light, and other forms of energy are generated and new substances can be formed. Exploring chemical reactions and their results is the work of the chemist.

Why are some fabrics absorbent?

Materials ❑ Large glass (8- or 10-ounce)
❑ Water
❑ Cotton handkerchief
❑ Small glass (4- or 6-ounce)

Procedure 1. Fill the large glass three-fourths full with water.
2. Completely immerse the handkerchief in the water.
3. Place the smaller glass next to the larger one.
4. Pull one end of the wet handkerchief out of the large glass and place it along the inside upper lip of the smaller glass. (See FIG. 13-1.)
5. Leave the glasses and the handkerchief in that position for about 12 hours.

13-1 Surface tension water movement

Results The *surface tension* of the water causes the *molecular* movement, or flow, of the water through the handkerchief. Because of this movement, the water flows from the larger glass into the smaller glass. In his youth, *Michael Faraday*, an English chemist, observed this movement of water. In Faraday's case, he had left a wash towel in a water basin during the night. The exposed end of the towel hung near the floor. The next day all of the water had drained from the water basin onto the floor.

Further studies Fabrics are made from a variety of *fibers*—long, thin threads that are spun and woven together. The fibers can be natural such as cotton, which comes from a plant, and wool, which comes from an animal (sheep). Or the fibers can be *synthetic* such as polyester and nylon, which are manufactured from chemicals. In this activity, try to determine which has more absorbency—natural or synthetic fibers.

First, obtain a handkerchief-sized piece of each of the following fabrics: cotton, wool, polyester, and nylon.

Place each piece of fabric in a glass of water. Then, follow steps 3 through 5 as above.

Based on your observations, which fabrics have the best absorbency—those made of natural or synthetic fibers? Can all of the fabrics move water from one glass to another? Which fabric moves the water the best? Which fabric moves the water the slowest? What does this comparison tell you about the absorbency of fabrics?

Did you know?
- Silk, a natural fiber, is spun by a special worm, the silkworm. Legend has it that the Chinese discovered the secret of the silkworm in 2640 B.C. Today as then, silk is prized for its bright colors and smooth feel.
- Wool and water make strange companions. Wool repels water, at first. But once wet, wool doesn't give up water and dry quickly. What's also interesting, wool can absorb 30 percent of its weight in moisture and not feel wet.

Why does soap make suds?

Materials
(FIG. 14-1)

☐ Two test tubes
☐ Water
☐ 5 ounces lye
☐ Candle
☐ Test tube holder
☐ Test tube stand
☐ Salt
☐ Butter
☐ Protective goggles
☐ Protective gloves

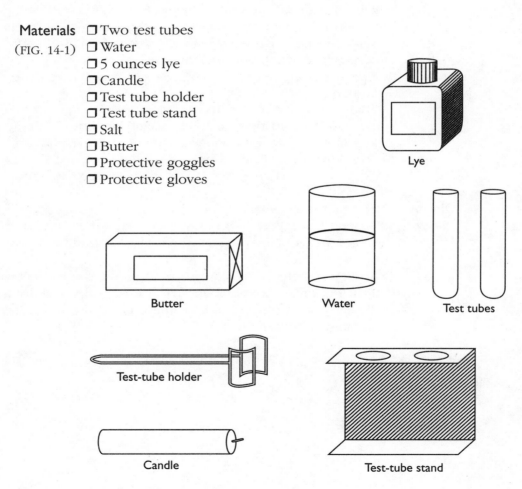

Lye

Butter

Water

Test tubes

Test-tube holder

Candle

Test-tube stand

14-1 Materials for making soap

Procedure

1. Fill one of the test tubes with ½ ounce (1 tablespoon) of water. Ask an adult to help you with the following steps.
2. Wearing protective goggles and gloves, carefully add 4 teaspoons of lye to the test tube.
3. Add about ½ teaspoon butter. Do not taste this mixture.
4. Carefully heat this mixture over the candle for several minutes. (See FIG. 14-2.) You can heat the mixture until the test tube blackens.
5. When the butter has completely dissolved, remove the test tube from the flame and add ¾ teaspoon of salt to the test tube.
6. Let the mixture cool; then, place your thumb over the test tube and shake. Be sure to wash your hands thoroughly after completing this step. Any unreacted lye is very caustic.
7. The soap will float to the top of the test tube.

Results When the soap has cooled, it can be removed from the top of the liquid. This soap can be tested for suds by placing a small amount of it in another test tube with some water and shaking the combination. Testing to make suds.

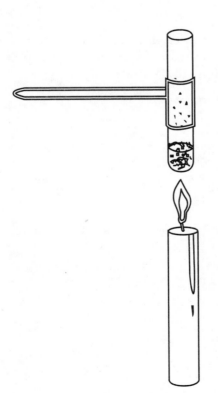

14-2 Heating the soap mixture

During soap's preparation, sodium carbonate, calcium oxide, and water combine to make sodium hydroxide (lye). The heated sodium hydroxide (lye) split the butter into a fatty acid and *glycerine*. After this split, the sodium reacted with the fatty acid to form soap. This sodium/fatty acid substance (soap) is called sodium stearate.

Soap can reduce water's *surface tension*. This reduction in surface tension makes the water more flexible. As a result, bubbles, or suds, can form and hold their shape.

Further studies

Many different types of soaps are made by combining metals with sodium stearate. Let's make one:

First, carefully dissolve ⅛ teaspoon ferric ammonium sulfate in ½ ounce of water in a test tube. Shake this solution until all of the metal is dissolved. Then, combine the metal solution with sodium stearate. Do not taste any of the chemicals.

Next, analyze your soap. What color is it? Does the soap make foam when it is shaken? What would you call this soap?

Did you know?

○ Ancient people washed themselves with ashes and water. Then they applied oil to their skin to counteract irritation from the ashes.
○ For centuries, the English and French peoples used perfume to cover up odor instead of washing with soap. In fact, soap was not widely used until the 17th century.

Why does metal rust?

Materials
- ❑ Large glass jar
- ❑ Water
- ❑ Two test tubes
- ❑ Iron powder

Procedure

1. Fill the jar with several ounces of water. This jar should be able to hold two inverted test tubes without them tipping over.
2. Fill one test tube with water and empty it out. Sprinkle a small amount of the iron powder into the bottom of the wet test tube. The iron should stick to the sides of the test tube.
3. Turn the test tube upside down and place it in the water-filled glass jar.
4. Place the other empty test tube in an inverted position next to the iron-filled one.
5. Let both of these test tubes sit undisturbed for several days. (See FIG. 15-1.)
6. Observe the results.

Results What happened to the water level inside the iron-filled test tube? Slowly, the iron powder began to rust. As the rust formed, the level of water in the test tube rose. This change was due to the consumption, or use of oxygen, from the air inside the test tube.

    As proof that the air didn't just leak out of the iron-filled test tube, check the second test tube, which served as a control. Its water level should be the same as it was when the experiment started. In other words, the second test tube duplicated all of the major actions of the experiment without actually duplicating the experiment itself.

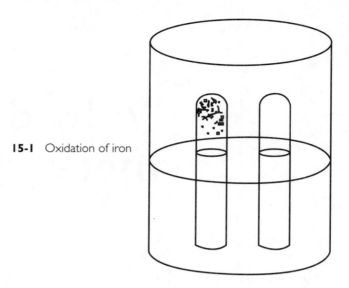

15-1 Oxidation of iron

The use of oxygen in this reaction is called *oxidation*. Oxidation is a chemical reaction that combines oxygen with another substance. When oxygen combines with the other substance, an oxide is formed. The rust on the iron powder is called iron oxide or ferric oxide (Fe_2O_3).

Further studies One way to prevent the oxidation of iron is to seal it from the influence of oxygen. Prepare an experiment that demonstrates this statement. Be sure to use controls in your experiment.

Did you know?
- Not all metals rust, or corrode. Gold and platinum stay bright and shiny no matter how long they're exposed to air and water.
- When copper oxidizes (corrodes), it turns from reddish brown to green. That's why the Statue of Liberty, which is made of copper, is green.

Why does litmus paper change colors?

Materials
(FIG. 16-1)

❏ Three pieces of red litmus paper
❏ One 8 ½-x-11-inch piece of paper
❏ Three pieces of blue litmus paper
❏ Ammonia
❏ Vinegar
❏ Distilled water
❏ Medicine dropper

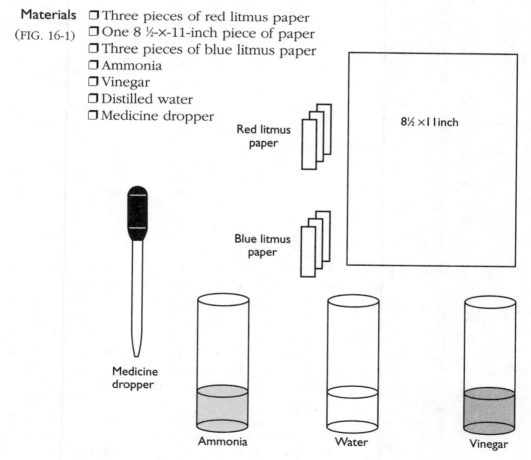

Red litmus paper

8½ ×11 inch

Blue litmus paper

Medicine dropper

Ammonia   Water   Vinegar

16-1 Materials for testing acids and bases

Procedure

1. For this experiment, work in a room with good ventilation.
2. Place the red litmus paper on the 8½- x-11-inch sheet of paper.
3. Write a label below each piece of litmus paper: water, ammonia, and vinegar.
4. Place the blue litmus paper on the same sheet of paper.
5. Again, write a label below each piece of litmus paper: water, ammonia, and vinegar.
6. With the medicine dropper, carefully place three drops of each liquid on the appropriate piece of litmus paper. In other words, place water on the litmus paper that has a water label and the vinegar on the paper labeled vinegar and so on. (See FIG. 16-2.) Do not taste the ammonia, and work cautiously so that you don't splash the vinegar or the ammonia.

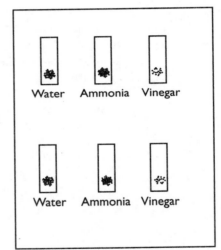

16-2 Litmus paper test

Results There are three types of chemical fluids: *neutral* liquids, *acids,* and *bases*. A neutral liquid doesn't change the color of *litmus* paper. A base will change red litmus paper to blue. An acid will change blue litmus paper to red. Based on this information, is ammonia an acid or a base? Likewise, is vinegar an acid or a base? How about water?

An acid contains a large portion of hydrogen (H^+) *ions*. Bases, on the other hand, contain hydroxyl (OH^-) ions. A neutral chemical has an equal number of these two ions (H^+ and OH^-).

Further studies What will happen when an acid and a base are mixed together? In a well-ventilated room, test your answer by carefully combining the acid and the base from the above experiment. Use red and blue litmus paper to monitor your progress. Remember not to splash the liquids and do not taste them.

1. Begin by filling a small glass jar with ¼ cup water.
2. Pour 1 tablespoon of the acid (vinegar) into another small jar.
3. Using the medicine dropper, add 1 or 2 drops of the vinegar to the water. Thoroughly mix the two liquids together.
4. Check the results on a piece of blue, then red litmus paper. Add another 3 or 4 drops of vinegar and test again.
5. Pour 1 tablespoon of the base (ammonia) into a third small jar.
6. Now, add 1 or 2 drops of the ammonia to the vinegar/water mixture. Test the results on blue, then red litmus paper.
7. Add another 2 drops of ammonia and test again. Add two more drops of ammonia and test again.

How much base do you have to add before the litmus paper doesn't change colors anymore? Check both litmus papers. Does either one make a color change in this final acid plus base solution? What is another name for the final solution? How does this solution relate to the three types of chemical fluids?

Did you know?
○ The dye for litmus paper comes from a unique source: lichens, composite organisms made up of fungi and algae. Lichens grow on harsh surfaces such as rocks, tree bark, and poor soil.
○ By combining vinegar and baking soda, you can observe a chemical reaction taking place. The mixture foams as carbon dioxide forms and disappears into the air.

Why does a lemon taste sour?

Materials
(FIG. 17-1)
❏ Knife
❏ Fresh lemon
❏ Galvanized zinc nail
❏ Penny

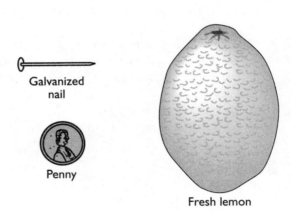

Galvanized
nail

Penny

Fresh lemon

17-1 Materials for making a simple wet-cell battery

Procedure

1. With the knife, very carefully make two short, parallel cuts in one end of the lemon. Remember to work on a cutting board or other cutting surface and to cut away from yourself.
2. Gently push the nail into one of the cuts.
3. Push the penny into the other cut.
4. Make sure that 1 inch of each metal is sticking out of the lemon.
5. Carefully and simultaneously place your tongue on both metals. (See FIG. 17-2.)

17-2 Simple wet-cell battery

Results The feeling that you experienced in your tongue is a slight trickle of electricity produced by the lemon's reaction to the zinc and copper. In order to produce electricity, three items must be present: an *electron*-rich metal, an *electron*-poor metal, and an *electrolyte*. The combination of these four items is known as a wet-cell battery. The lemon with the zinc and copper has all four of these items. Therefore, the lemon can be thought of as a wet-cell battery.

Use a piece of red and a piece of blue litmus paper to test the lemon's juice. Is the lemon juice an acid or a base? The acid found in a lemon is citric acid. The large amount of citric acid in lemons contributes to their sour taste.

During the production of electricity, the water and citric acid in the lemon release electrons. This water/acid solution is called the electrolyte. The zinc then collects these electrons. Both of the metals are called *electrodes*. Zinc is the negative electrode and the copper is the positive electrode. In turn, the copper or copper electrode is able to receive electrons.

Any direct connection between the zinc and copper electrodes will cause the copper to receive these needed electrons. Your tongue serves as this connection. The movement of the electrons between the two electrodes is called electricity. Once the copper electrode has received its electrons, they are sent back to the zinc electrode through the electrolyte. This reaction will continue until one of the four items is used up.

Further studies Many fruits and some vegetables can be used to make a simple wet-cell battery. Evaluate several fruits and vegetables: orange, grapefruit, apple, pear, potato, tomato, and cucumber. Which fruit produces the greatest amount of electricity? Which vegetable makes the best wet-cell battery?

Other metals can also be used as the electrodes. Try substituting iron, tin, or aluminum for the zinc. Then using the zinc, try substituting each one for the copper. Which of these metals makes the best electrode? Which electrode should these metals be used for—the positive or negative electrode? What metal did you use for the other electrode?

Did you know?

○ Although Thomas Edison is generally credited with the invention of the lightbulb, he was not the first. Joseph Swan of England actually patented an electric lamp using carbon for the filament in 1878; Edison did not patent his invention until 1879. Edison, however, was the first to develop incandescent lighting for the home and for street lamps. Although Edison and Swan at first argued about who owned the patent, they later started an electric company together.

○ Neon (from the Greek meaning "new") is a colorless, odorless gas used in neon lighting. The gas was discovered in 1898 by two English chemists, William Ramsey and Morris Travers. In nature, neon gas has red-orange glow. Neon lighting, such as that used in the brilliant lights of Las Vegas, Nevada, gets its color by altering the gas and placing powders inside the tube.

Why is invisible ink invisible?

Materials
(FIG. 18-1)

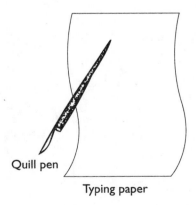

☐ Lemon
☐ Small glass jar
☐ Clean quill pen
☐ White typing paper
☐ Iron
☐ Old towel

Fresh lemon

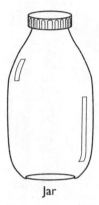

Jar

Quill pen

Typing paper

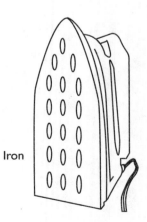

Iron

18-1 Materials for making invisible ink

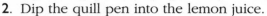

Procedure 1. Squeeze the lemon and let the juice drip into the small glass jar.

2. Dip the quill pen into the lemon juice.
3. Write with the pen on the white typing paper.
4. Let the lemon juice message dry.
5. With the help of an adult, turn on the iron. Use a dry setting on high (cotton).
6. Turn your message over so that it's on the back side of the paper. On the old towel, iron your message, quickly and carefully. **Do not leave the iron on the paper for long**. (See FIG. 18-2.) The iron will be very hot and can burn you as well as your paper. Be sure you do this step with an adult's assistance.

Results The lemon juice ink turned dark brown when it was heated. This change from the clear, or invisible condition, to the visible brown color is similar to the action seen in pieces of cut fruit such as apples, pears, and peaches. When fruit pieces are exposed to air, they age (oxide) and turn brown.

18-2 Writing with invisible ink

If the cut fruit is dipped in lemon juice, however, the juice can slow the browning because it contains citric acid. The citric acid acts as a preservative. But if citric acid is removed, even lemon juice will turn brown. In this experiment, the heat from the iron destroyed the citric acid and left the lemon juice ready for aging and changing color.

Further studies   You can make invisible ink from at least one other common food. Can you guess which one? For starters, why not try milk or orange, pineapple, grapefruit, or apple juice? To test each one, follow the procedure for the lemon juice ink.

Which of these beverage inks becomes invisible when dry? When heated, which turns brown so you can read your secret message?

Did you know?
- Bases are sometimes called alkalies. *Alkalie* comes from the Arabic word meaning "ashes of a plant." Most plants contain chemicals that can be made into bases. Centuries ago, people made bases by adding water to ashes in a fire.
- A shortage of fats during World War II encouraged the development of soapless detergents. Since 1965, all detergents made in the United States are biodegradeable, which means that they break down into products that are harmless to the environment.

Part 4
The Young Meteorologist

A recent survey reported that the most frequently asked question among a group of people was, "What is the weather going to be like tomorrow?" This unusual survey result reflects the importance of weather to the average person. *Meteorology* is the study of weather and its effects on the atmosphere. Meteorologists try to predict future weather patterns based on observations of current conditions. These observations, as well as the resulting *forecast*, or future weather predictions, are based on several of the other sciences. Chemistry, life sciences, and physics all play a major role in the effectiveness of meteorology.

Experiment 19

Why can meteorologists predict weather?

Materials
❏ Outdoor thermometer
❏ Barometer
❏ Daily newspaper
❏ Pencil
❏ Notebook

Procedure
1. Study the weather conditions in your city. Make a weather observation at a regular time each day for a week.
2. Record your weather observations for that period.
3. Each evening, read the weather summary in a local daily newspaper.
4. Add this information to your daily weather record.
5. On the seventh day, predict what the weather will be like on the eighth day.
6. Be sure to include *predictions* for high temperature, low temperature, wind direction, wind speed, and cloud conditions. (See FIG. 19-1.)

Results
How accurate was your prediction? The key to an accurate weather *forecast* is numerous daily observations of temperature, moisture, *barometric pressure*, and wind. These observations supply you with *atmospheric data* that you must correctly interpret. If you have good data for each of these weather factors, then you can predict the next day's weather.

Further studies
Repeat this experiment, but this time study only the four weather prediction factors. Remember moisture includes both *precipitation*

Day	1	2	3	4	5	6	7	Prediction
Weather Conditions								
Temperature								
High								
Low								
Wind								
Direction								
Speed								
Barometric Pressure								
Relative Humidity								
Cloud								
Type								
Conditions								

19-1 Weather prediction chart

and humidity. How accurate was your prediction this time? Was it more accurate than last time? Another factor that will also affect forecasting is experience in reading current weather data and predicting future weather conditions. Gain experience in predicting weather by repeating this experiment for a month. Do your predictions increase in their accuracy through the month?

Did you know?

○ Al Aziziyah in western Libya holds the world record for the hottest temperature—136°F in the shade. And a Soviet research station Vostok in Anarctica earns the coldest recorded temperature award: −127°F.

○ Chili's Atacama Desert is the driest region in the world. Parts of this desert have known no rain. In contrast, Mount Waialeale in Hawaii sees rain 350 days a year and gets about 450 inches of the wet stuff.

Why do you hear thunder?

Materials   ❏ Stopwatch or watch that displays seconds

Procedure
1. From inside a building, watch for a bolt of lightning from a distant summer thunderstorm. If the storm comes close, shut the window and move away from it. Do not go outside during a thunderstorm.
2. As soon as you see the lightning's flash, start your stopwatch, or start watching the seconds on your watch.
3. When you hear the clap of thunder, stop the stopwatch.
4. Determine the number of seconds that it took the thunder's sound to reach your position.
5. Divide that number of seconds by 5.
6. The resulting value is the lightning's distance, in miles, from your position.

Results   A severe thunderstorm usually consists of both lightning and thunder. The sound of the thunder travels more slowly than the light from the lightning. Light from lightning moves at 186,000 miles per second, while the clap from the thunder travels at 1,100 miles per second. Therefore, the sound of the thunder reaches your location considerably later than the visual sighting of the lightning.

Lightning is produced by electrically charged clouds coming into near contact with the ground. The charging in a storm cloud is due to the movement of positive and negative rain drops within the cloud. When this movement has reached the potential of the cloud, an electric spark results. This spark is seen as lightning. As the lightning bolts toward the ground, the surrounding air is heated. This heated air expands explosively and generates a clap of thunder.

Further studies Using the technique you just learned for calculating your distance from a thunderstorm, plot the track of the thunderstorm. How does the shape of the lightning and the sound of the thunder change during the storm's movement? Can you determine the location of the storm based on the shape of the lightning? Likewise, can you determine a storm's rough location based on just the sound of the thunder?

Did you know?
○ A streak of lightning is four or more times hotter than the sun's surface. With a blast of heat that's 27,000°F or more, lightning can explode trees and melt sand.
○ Hailstones, pellets of ice produced by violent thunderstorms, come in assorted sizes. Most are grape or walnut size, but some get to be as big as tennis balls. The largest hailstone ever recorded had a diameter of 5½ inches and weighed 1½ pounds.

Why is humidity so uncomfortable?

Materials ❒ Two Celsius thermometers
❒ Masking tape
❒ One 3- × -6-inch piece of cardboard
❒ Two rubber bands
❒ 8-inch piece of string
❒ 2-inch square of muslin

Procedure 1. Securely tape the two thermometers parallel to each other on the piece of cardboard. The bulb ends of both thermometers should extend over the edge of the cardboard. Additionally, the bulb end of one thermometer should extend out further than the end of the other thermometer. (See FIG. 21-1.)

2. Punch a hole in the cardboard in the end that is farthest from the thermometer bulbs.

3. Put the string through this hole, and tie it in a strong knot.

4. Wrap the muslin tightly around the thermometer bulb that extends furthest out from the cardboard.

5. Hold the muslin in place with the two rubber bands.

6. Dip the muslin in some water.

7. Spin the *psychrometer* over your head for 1 minute.

8. Read the temperatures from both thermometers. Record these values as a dry-bulb temperature (the thermometer reading without the muslin) and a wet-bulb temperature (the thermometer reading with the muslin). The difference between these two temperatures is the wet-bulb depression.

9. Use TABLE 21-1 to determine the relative humidity based on the air temperature and the wet-bulb depression.

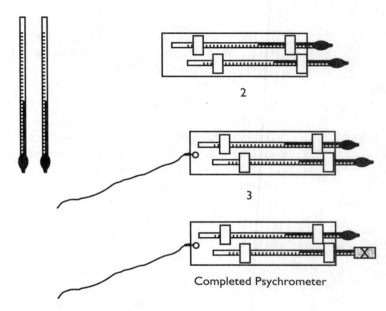

21-1 Constructing a psychrometer

Table 21-1. Relative Humidity

Wet-bulb depression	1	2	3	4	5	6	7	8	9
Dry-bulb Temperature									
−5	76	52	29	7	–	–	–	–	
0	81	64	46	29	13	–	–	–	–
5	86	72	58	45	33	20	7	–	–
10	88	77	66	55	44	34	24	15	6
15	90	80	71	61	53	44	36	27	20
20	91	83	74	66	59	51	44	37	31
25	92	84	77	70	63	57	50	44	39
30	93	86	79	73	67	61	55	50	44
35	94	87	81	75	69	64	59	54	49

Results *Relative humidity* determines our comfort. A high relative humidity in the summer months makes you feel sticky because *perspiration* cannot *evaporate* from your skin quickly. On the other hand, too little *humidity* in the winter months can dry out your skin and cause discomfort in breathing.

Relative humidity is used to determine the amount of moisture in the air. This moisture content can reach an extreme when there is too much moisture for the air to hold. At this point, the air is *saturated* (filled) with water *vapor,* and *dew* forms if the temperature falls.

The warmer the air is, the more water vapor it can hold. A decrease in temperature means that the air can hold less water. The temperature at which dew begins to form for a certain amount of water vapor is called the *dew point*.

When the dew point is equal to or lower than the air temperature, the air stays saturated. As the air temperature falls nearer the dew point, the saturated water vapor *condenses* into water droplets. These water droplets form on any object that is surrounded by cool air. The cool air is the trigger for making dew.

Let's look at the way dew forms in typical summer weather. During the warm day, the air fills with water vapor. As night comes, the air cools. But the cooler air cannot hold as much water as the warmer daytime air. What happens? The excess water vapor forms tiny drops, or dew, on windows, blades of grass, picnic tables.

Further studies Investigate the formation of dew. Go outside on a morning after a heavy dew has formed. Look for objects that have dew on them. Which objects don't have any dew on them? What are several characteristics of these objects without dew? Can you make a deduction about the formation of dew based on these observations?

Did you know?
○ The dog days of summer are very hot, humid days that are marked by the appearance of the star Sirius in the July and August night sky. Sirius is also called the dog star. Hence the name dog days of summer.
○ The air above you is a very heavy weight on your shoulders. In fact, it exerts about a ton of downward pressure. Why don't you feel it? Because you're being held up by an equal amount of atmospheric pressure on all sides.

Experiment 22

Why do clouds have different shapes?

Materials ❏ Pencil
  ❏ Notebook

Procedure 1. Study the clouds for several days.
  2. In your notebook, make several sketches of the different cloud formations that you see. Write a brief description of each cloud formation.
  3. Check a local daily newspaper for weather conditions on each day that you observed the clouds.
  4. Record the weather information in your notebook with your sketched cloud formations.

Results Clouds form from the *condensation* of saturated water vapor. This condensation is caused by changes in temperature. For example, a cloud formation will develop when a warm, saturated air mass moves over a cooler ground surface. Conversely, a cloud formation will develop when a cool air mass flows over a warm surface. Once the cloud has formed, its shape is changed by air currents and by evaporation from contact with unsaturated air masses.

In 1803, Luke Howard discovered four general cloud types: *cirrus, cumulus, nimbus,* and *stratus.* Cirrus clouds are high-altitude white clouds. The lower-altitude, fluffy white clouds are cumulus clouds. Nimbus clouds are the gray rain clouds that lack shape and usually blanket the sky. Finally, extremely low-altitude, thin, billowy clouds are stratus clouds. (See FIG. 22-1.)

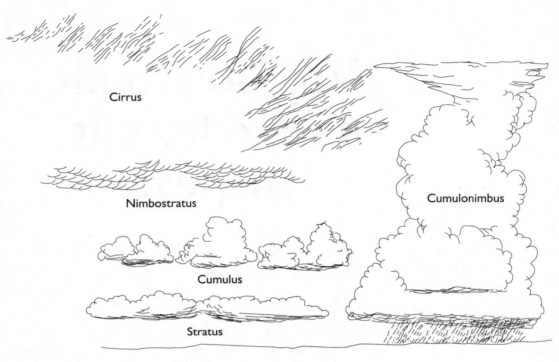

Cirrus

Nimbostratus

Cumulonimbus

Cumulus

Stratus

22-1 Some common cloud types

Further studies Based on the descriptions of the four general cloud types, classify, or name, the clouds that you observed. Did you see all four types? Which types of clouds were the most numerous? What was the weather with each type of cloud?

Did you know?
○ The U.S. National Weather Service was founded February 9, 1870.
○ The U.S. Weather Bureau used to label a high-altitude, non-storm cloud as cloud nine.

Part 5
The Young Biologist

Biologists delve into a number of fields of study collectively called the life sciences. *Biology, botany, ecology, genetics, microbiology, physiology,* and *zoology* are all sciences under the life sciences name. Each of the science fields, or branches, retains its own identity. For example, ecology is the science of animal populations and the environment. The life sciences classification unites ecology along with all of the other individual branches into one central category. The combination facilitates the exchange of information among the life sciences branches.

Why do plants have leaves?

Materials ❏ Thin cardboard
❏ One house plant
❏ Paper clip

Procedure 1. Cut two ½- to ¾-inch circles from the cardboard.
2. Place one of these circles on either side of a growing plant leaf. Do not remove the leaf from the plant, and do not taste the leaf.
3. Use the paper clip to hold the two circles in position.
4. Set the plant in normal sunlight.
5. After four days, remove the cardboard circles. (See FIG. 23-1.)

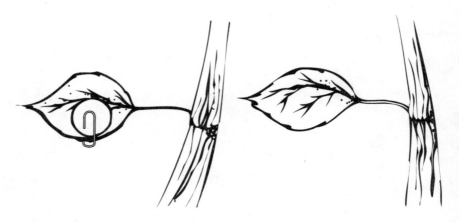

23-1 Testing photosynthesis

Results When you removed the cardboard circles, the area under them looked lighter in color than the rest of the leaf. In some cases, the area may have looked yellowish. The color difference was due to the lack of *chlorophyll* production in the covered area.

Chlorophyll is a green food-producing substance that is found in plant leaves. This food production from chlorophyll is started by light striking the leaf. The light-into-food process is called *photosynthesis*.

Many of the nutrients that we commonly have in our food are produced by the photosynthetic action of many leaves. For example, the food contained inside one apple is produced by the photosynthesis of 50 apple tree leaves.

The production of this food from a leaf can be thought of as a small oven that uses the cooking ingredients of chlorophyll and sunlight. Combining chlorophyll with sunlight makes the photosynthetic action that removes carbon from the water and air and produces starch and sugar. It is this starch and sugar that are the food products of the leaf.

Further studies Here are two more activities you can do with leaves:

Create a catalog of the plants in your yard. Being careful not to pick poison ivy, oak, or sumac leaves—which can cause a very itchy rash on your skin—collect a leaf from each plant in the yard. Place each leaf between two sheets of waxed paper, and stack several heavy books on top of this leaf-paper sandwich. After several days, the leaf should be dried and pressed. Now, tape this leaf carefully to a sheet of colored construction paper.

To identify each leaf, use a leaf guide such as *Trees: A Guide to Familiar American Trees* by Herbert S. Zim, PhD., ScD. and Alexander C. Martin, PhD.; *A Field Guide to Trees and Shrubs* by George A. Petrides; *Flowers: A Guide to Familiar American Wildflowers* by Herbert S. Zim, PhD., ScD. and Alexander C. Martin, PhD.; or *A Field Guide to Wildflowers of Northeastern and Northcentral North America* by Roger Tory Peterson and Margaret McKenny.

Write the plant's name at the top of the paper. Keep the papers in a folder.

Create a leaf design on a T-shirt. For the design, you need a large, leaf with obvious veins. Leaves from these trees work well: oak, maple, sassafras, and tuliptree. (See FIG. 23-2.) Do not pick leaves from poison ivy, oak, or sumac because you could get a nasty, itchy rash. (See FIG. 23-3.) After you have found a suitable leaf, do the following:

1. Place the leaf on a flat surface.
2. Color one side of the leaf with a crayon. You may use any color. Be careful that you don't tear or break the leaf as you color it.

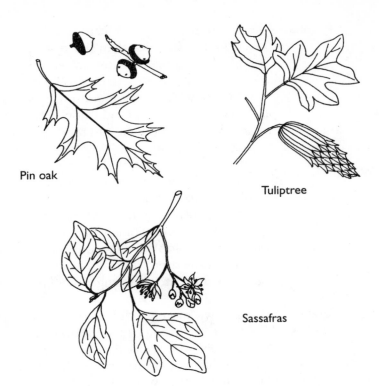

Pin oak

Tuliptree

Sassafras

23-2 Some common leaves.

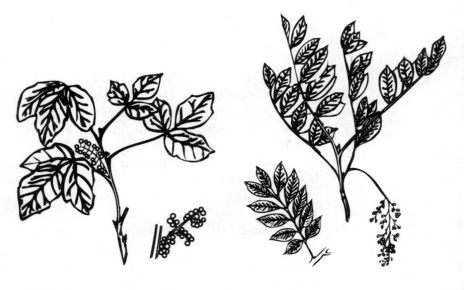

23-3 (Left to right) Poison ivy, oak, and sumac

3. Lay the crayon-colored side of the leaf on the front of your T-shirt.
4. Cover the leaf with a clean piece of waxed paper, and place an old towel on top of the paper.
5. With an adult's help, carefully heat an iron to medium (on a dry setting), and holding the iron's handle, gently iron the leaf. Do not touch the metal part of the iron. It will be hot and can burn you.
6. The iron's heat will melt the crayon wax and leave the shape of the leaf on your T-shirt. This type of T-shirt is NOT suitable for machine washing. Hand wash your leaf T-shirt in cold water, or the crayon image will wash out.

Did you know? ○ Only the tuber of the potato plant is edible. All other parts leaves, stems, and berries are poisonous.

Why do plants need light?

Materials ❏ Two 4-inch flower pots
❏ Potting soil or loose dirt
❏ One package bush beans

Procedure 1. Fill each pot with soil. Plant a bean seed ½ inch down in each pot. Keep the soil moist until the seeds *germinate*, or sprout.

2. Grow the plants in normal sunlight for several weeks until the plants are at least 12 inches tall. Remember to water the plants as they need it.

3. Place one of the bean plants in a dark closet where no sunlight can strike the plant.

4. Place the other bean plant in normal sunlight.

5. Water and care for the plants on a regular basis. Make sure that no sunlight reaches the bean plant in the closet when you care for the plant.

6. After two weeks, remove the bean plant from the closet.

7. Compare the two plants.

Results Plants that are kept in the dark lose their green color because they can't produce chlorophyll without sunlight. Light is also important to a plant for the production of its food. This food is made by photosynthesis, which is the reaction of chlorophyll with sunlight.

In addition to making food, a plant also *consumes* food. Food consumption in a plant is called *respiration*. When food production is removed from a plant— for example, through the loss of light—the plant continues to respire or use food. Usually the plant will take the needed food from itself. Therefore, by using food while not making food, the plant is actually consuming itself. The result is that the plant begins to lose color and will eventually die.

Further studies Continue testing the value of light on your bean plants. Take the bean plant that was in the closet and leave it in normal sunlight. Conversely, place the bean plant from normal sunlight in the dark closet. Water and care for both plants. In several weeks, observe the results. Did the plants change color? Has the bean plant originally from the closet fully recovered?

Now, leave both plants in normal sunlight. Water and care for the plants. After several weeks, can you tell which plant is which?

Did you know?
○ Molds and mushrooms have no chlorophyll; so they can't manufacture their own food. How do they survive? By living off other plants and animals, both living and dead.
○ Lichens, those tiny composite plants of algae and fungi, can live to a very ripe old age. Some of the rock-covering types in the Arctic are roughly 4,500 years old.

Why do plants have roots?

Materials   ❏ One 4-inch flower pot
❏ Potting soil or loose dirt
❏ One package bush beans
❏ Small glass jar
❏ Red food coloring

Procedure   1. Fill the pot with soil. Plant a bean seed ½ inch down in the pot. Keep the soil moist until the seed germinates, or sprouts.
2. Grow the plant in normal sunlight for several weeks until the plant is approximately 6 inches tall. Remember to water the plant.
3. Place the plant in a dark closet for 2 weeks. Continue to water and care for the plant during this time.
4. Remove the plant from the closet.
5. Gently remove the bean plant from its planter. Carefully shake the dirt from the plant's roots; then rinse the entire plant in water to remove any remaining dirt.
6. Fill the glass jar with tap water.
7. Add several drops of red food coloring to the water. The water should be a bright red color.
8. Lower the bean plant's roots into the red water.
9. Leave the plant in the water for several hours.

Note: If you have trouble seeing any color change in this experiment, place a celery stalk in the red water and leave it for several hours.

Results   The root system of a plant pulls water and nutrients from the soil. In this experiment, the water traveled from the bean plant's roots (or the celery stalk) to the leaves and turned the leaves pink.

Small root hairs are responsible for absorbing water and *nutrients* from the soil. This water eventually enters the root's outer *cor-*

tex layer. From the cortex, the water moves to the center of the root called the center cylinder. The center cylinder is composed of hundreds of small cells that carry the water and nutrients upward by *capillary action,* the movement of a liquid in a narrow tube.

Further studies
You can also study the movement of a liquid by doing a comparison of paper towels. First, get several different brands of paper towels. Then dip a corner of one towel from each brand into a dish of water. Which pulls up the water the fastest? Which the highest? What is the width of the capillary action?

Did you know?
○ Water travels from a plant's roots to its leaves at remarkable speeds. In some trees, the speed approaches 100 miles an hour.
○ Incredibly deep roots hold up some plants. Big, old hickory and oak trees, for example, have tap roots that extend down as much as 100 feet. And alfalfa roots can reach down 30 feet.

Why is the ocean salty?

Materials
- ❏ 282 grams sodium chloride
- ❏ 17 grams calcium sulfate
- ❏ 10 liters water
- ❏ 32 grams magnesium sulfate
- ❏ 8 grams magnesium chloride
- ❏ 8 grams potassium chloride
- ❏ 1 gram magnesium bromide
- ❏ Large glass jar
- ❏ Lid to fit the jar

Procedure
1. Add the sodium chloride and the calcium chloride to 3 liters of the water.
2. Stir this mixture until the two chemicals dissolve.
3. Place the lid on the jar.
4. Shake this mixture.
5. Add the remaining chemicals.
6. Add the final 7 liters of water.
7. Stir this mixture until all of the chemicals dissolve.

Results   You have just made the standard sea water mixture used by the world's leading marine aquariums. Many of these institutions supplement their artificial sea water with small quantities of actual sea water. This step is necessary to provide the captive marine creatures with the numerous trace elements that can't be adequately duplicated with synthetic compounds.

   The sodium, potassium, calcium, and magnesium chemical compounds used in this artificial sea water preparation are all salts. When combined with water, they make the water salty.

Further studies As a test of your artificial sea water, create a saltwater aquarium. Use only a high-quality, all-glass aquarium to hold your miniature ocean because the saltwater solution is highly corrosive and can damage slate and metal aquarium tanks.

Cover the bottom of the tank with clean sand and gravel. If possible, boil the sand and gravel in water, then pour off the water before putting the sand mixture in the tank. Finally, fill the aquarium tank with your artificial sea water.

The true test of your newly created ocean is whether it will support marine plant and animal life. Obtain several simple plant and invertebrate animal samples from a scientific supply house, or take a field trip to the seashore and make your own collection. Once the creatures have been placed inside the tank, add an aerator and a temperature-control element, as needed. This need is based on the type of environment that the plants and animals originally called home.

Did you know?

○ Because salt water is heavier than fresh water, it has greater *buoyancy*, which makes it easier to swim or float in the ocean than in a fresh-water lake. The Great Salt Lake in Utah has so much salt in it that you can't sink or completely submerge yourself.

○ Salt accumulates in deep basins that have been cut off from the rest of the ocean. As the seawater evaporates, salt *precipitates* out of the water and drops to the sea bed. Since salt deposits have been found as far north as the Arctic Circle, scientists know that either the region used to be closer to the equator, or that the climate was a great deal warmer than it is now. Such deposits also indicate that New Mexico was once under water, and that the Gulf of Mexico and the Mediterranean sea were once completely dry.

Why should a houseplant be rotated?

Materials
❐ Two 4-inch flower pots
❐ Potting soil or loose dirt
❐ One package bush beans

Procedure
1. Fill the flower pots with soil. Plant a seed ½ inch down in the soil in each pot. Keep the soil moist until the seeds germinate, or sprout.
2. Grow the plants for several weeks until they are about 12 inches tall. Remember to water them.
3. Find a sunny window and place the pots in the sunlight.
4. Rotate one of the bean plants every day. Don't touch the other pot.
5. Continue to water both plants in a normal manner.

Results
The plant that was never rotated will be bent toward the sunlight. Conversely, the other bean plant will have a reasonably straight stem. The movement of a plant toward sunlight is called *phototropism*.

Without sunlight, a plant is unable to produce sufficient food for living. Therefore, a plant is capable of moving itself to gain the maximum benefit from its exposure to sunlight.

Further studies
A plant's stem is extremely flexible. Try these phototropic experiments with your two bean plants: First, switch your rotation plan. In this case, rotate the bean plant that was kept from the sunlight and don't rotate the straight-stemmed bean plant. What happened to the shape of each bean plant?

Leave the bean plant that you haven't rotated in the sunlight for several more days. How far will the stem bend? Can you correct this shape by rotating the plant? How long can you leave the plant before rotation will no longer straighten the stem?

Another effect on plants is *geotropism*. Geotropism is the movement that gravity causes a plant to exhibit. Here is a simple experiment that demonstrates geotropism: Set one of your bean pots on its side and leave the other one in a normal upright position. Be sure that you water and care for both of these plants during this experiment.

After several days, what is happening to the two plants? How does a plant react to gravity? Why is this response important to a plant?

Did you know?
○ Bamboo is an extremely fast-growing plant. It can put on as many as 3 feet a day.
○ Some Arctic lichens take hundreds of years to grow just one inch.

Why does a leaf sprout roots?

Materials
- ❏ African violet
- ❏ Small glass jar
- ❏ Water
- ❏ African violet plant fertilizer
- ❏ Waxed paper
- ❏ Rubber band

Procedure

1. Carefully break a leaf with at least a 2-inch stem from a full-grown African violet plant. Do not taste the leaf.
2. Fill the jar with water and carefully add fertilizer according to the instructions on the label. Do not taste the fertilizer; it could make you sick.
3. Cover the opening of the jar with the waxed paper. Fasten the waxed paper with the rubber band.
4. With a sharp pencil, gently poke a hole in the waxed paper. Insert the stem end of the African violet through the waxed paper. The stem should be at least 1 inch under the water's surface. Set the jar and leaf in normal sunlight.
5. Leave the stem in this position for several weeks. Replace the water and fertilizer as the water level decreases. (See FIG. 28-1.)

Results
A root system will slowly form on the African violet's stem. Once these roots are fully formed, you can transplant the leaf to a 4-inch flower pot filled with African violet potting soil.

To help the newly planted leaf and soil stay moist, create a mini-greenhouse over the leaf. Using a rubber band, attach a small plastic bag in a tent fashion over the top of the pot. (See FIG. 28-2.) Keep the soil moist, and avoid placing the plant in direct sun. Remove the

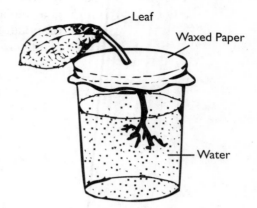

28-1 Allow the stem to stand in the water for several weeks.

Leaf

Waxed Paper

Water

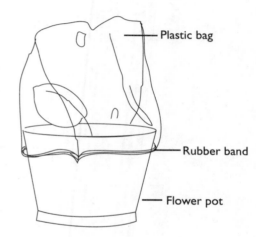

28-2 Mini-greenhouse over a newly planted leaf.

Plastic bag

Rubber band

Flower pot

plastic after one to two weeks, and water the plant regularly. In a year or two, this new African violet will be able to bloom.

Further studies Several types of plants can be started from leaf cuttings. Try starting other houseplants from leaf cuttings. One houseplant that you might try is the geranium.

Follow the procedure described above. How long did it take the geranium leaf to sprout roots? Compare the root systems of the African violet leaf and the geranium leaf. Are they similar?

Now try this leaf cutting technique with another houseplant such as a philodendron. Can this leaf sprout roots? What does its root structure tell you about plants grown from cuttings?

Did you know? ○ Potatoes have eyes. Actually each so-called eye, or small white bump, is a miniature leaf with tiny buds. Cut out the eye with a chunk of potato; then plant the piece. Let it grow into a new potato plant.

Why do flowers make pollen?

Materials
❏ Four sheets of black construction paper
❏ Hand-held magnifying lens

Procedure

1. Divide each sheet of paper into 1-inch squares. (See FIG. 29-1.)
2. Find four flowering plants in your neighborhood.
3. Hold a sheet of the black construction paper underneath one or two flowers on each plant. (Note: Use a different sheet of paper for each plant.)
4. Carefully bend the flower over so that it is directly over the sheet of black construction paper.
5. Shake the flower.
6. Use the magnifying lens to make a rough count of the *pollen* produced by the plant. To make this pollen estimate, count all of the pollen grains within a single 1-inch square. Then multiply this number by the number of squares that contain pollen. (See FIG. 29-1).
7. Repeat this procedure for the other flowers.

Results
Pollen is a yellow grain that is produced by plants for making seeds. The pollen is produced in a plant's flower. Inside the flower, small sacks called anthers actually make the pollen. The anthers are the male reproductive organs of the flower. The flower's female reproductive organs are called stigma.

To make seeds, pollen must be transferred from the anthers to the stigma. The process is called *pollination*. From the stigma, pollen goes to the flower's ovary. Once in the ovary, an egg is *fertilized* by the pollen and a seed develops.

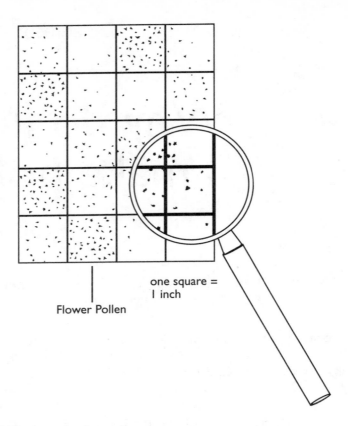

29-1   Collecting pollen from a flower

Plants depend on insects, birds, and the wind for pollination. And large amounts of pollen must be produced to ensure a successful pollination. Some plants, like corn, are able to produce 50 million pollen grains. Happy pollen-grain counting!

Further studies   Can you *artificially* pollinate a flower? Use a small camel-hair brush to pick up pollen grains from a flower's anthers. Place these pollen grains on the stigma of another flower. (See FIG. 29-2.) Make sure that this second flower is from a similar plant, but not the same plant as the pollen-producing flower. Now cover the flower that you just pollinated with a small plastic bag. Loosely secure this bag with a twist tie and move the plant out of direct sunlight.

Did the pollinated flower eventually produce any seeds? Plant these seeds. Did the seeds grow into a plant?

Master gardeners and researchers use artificial pollination to grow their own special plant breeds. They keep accurate records of

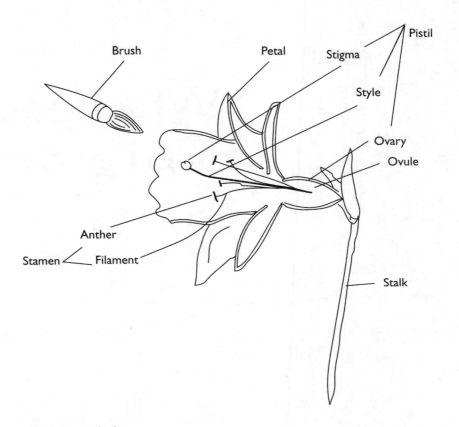

29-2 Parts of a flower

The plants they are artificially pollinating. It takes several years of work to develop new plant breeds, or varieties.

Did you know?
○ World-wide, more than 235,000 plant types produce seeds.
○ A plant in Southeast Asia, Rafflesia, produces giant blossoms up to 3 feet in diameter. Such big blooms aren't light-weights. Each weighs more than 10 pounds.

Why does mold grow?

Materials
- ❏ Water
- ❏ One glass jar with a wide mouth
- ❏ Wire such as a clothes hanger
- ❏ One-quarter slice of bread
- ❏ Waxed paper
- ❏ Rubber band
- ❏ Hand-held magnifying lens

Procedure

1. Put approximately ½ inch of water in the bottom of the jar.
2. Press one end of the wire through the bread.
3. Bend the other end of the wire into a hook.
4. Hook the wire over the mouth of the glass jar. The bread should hang inside the jar. (See FIG. 30-1.)
5. Cover the jar with waxed paper. Use a rubber band around the jar's opening to hold the waxed paper in place.
6. Observe the bread every day for several weeks. Look at it closely with your magnifying lens. Do not taste the bread. And handle it carefully so you don't spread the mold. Save the moldy bread for use in *Further studies*.

Results After several weeks, mold will form on the bread. Mold is a simple fungus that obtains its food from rotting fruits, vegetables, and flesh. Unlike other plants, mold does not have any *chlorophyll*. This lack of chlorophyll means that molds must use the food produced by other plants or animals.

    The mold that you see on your bread has many different colors. Black, white, and blue are several mold colors that form easily on bread. The diversity in color is due to the *spore* color. A spore is the small seed that produces the adult mold.

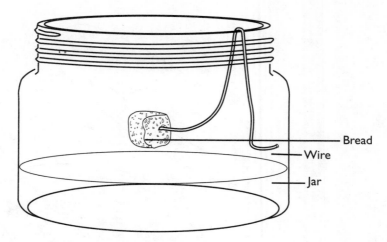

30-1 Creating an environment for growing mold

Once a spore lands on a suitable *culture*, or food host, an enormous network of threads called *hyphae* develops. If a hypha attaches to the culture, the hypha becomes a root. Mold hyphae that become roots are called *rhizoids*.

A hypha can also grow above the culture medium. A hypha that grows above a food source's surface is called a *stolon*. The mold's stolon is able to produce a *sporangium,* which is a spore sack. When the sporangium matures, it breaks and releases thousands of new spores. They start the mold-growing process all over again.

Further studies

Using the technique you learned for growing mold on bread, try growing mold on different fruits and vegetables. You might have to help the formation of mold on certain fruits and vegetables. One way to start mold growth is to bruise the fruit or vegetable by rolling it firmly on a hard surface. Which fruit or vegetable grows the most interesting looking mold?

Next, you can try isolating a mold on an artificial culture medium. Ask an adult to help you prepare the culture by combining 1 cup water, ¼ cup sugar, and 1 to 2 tbsp. cornstarch in a medium-sized saucepan. Bring the mixture to a boil. Cook just enough to dissolve the sugar and cornstarch. If the sugar and cornstarch don't dissolve, add more water. Add 1 packet of plain gelatin to the mixture and pour everything into a new, disposable, plastic petri dish. Cover and let your culture medium sit until it is cool. The gelatin will cause the culture medium to harden as it cools. (See FIG. 30-2.)

When the culture medium is ready, heat a long piece of wire in the flame of a match. This practice sterilizes the wire. After the wire

Why does mold grow? 87

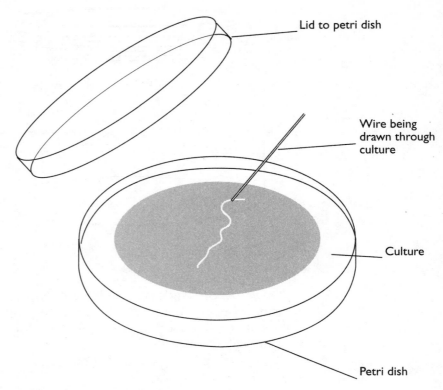

Lid to petri dish

Wire being drawn through culture

Culture

Petri dish

30-2 Growing mold in a petri dish

has cooled, dip the wire into a mold sample from the moldy bread from your first experiment. Drag the mold lightly across the surface of your culture medium and cover the dish. Observe the dish daily for about a week.

What happened to the culture medium? Did the mold sample grow? Did only one color of mold form? Was your mold sample pure? If your sample is multi-colored, it has more than one mold.

 Remember, do not taste mold or moldy food. Wash your hands after handling the petri dish. When the experiment is complete, throw the petri dish away.

Did you know?
○ Molds give blue cheeses and Roquefort cheese their distinctive, tangy flavors and marbled appearance.
○ The antibiotic penicillin is produced by a helpful mold.

Why do scientists save specimens?

Materials
- ❏ Collection equipment
- ❏ Specimens
- ❏ Mounting supplies
- ❏ Display cases
- ❏ Labels

Procedure

1. Determine the type of specimens that you wish to collect. This may include rocks and minerals, butterflies, tree leaves, or bird feathers.

2. Obtain the correct equipment for collecting your specimens. The following lists will be useful for the above specimens:

Rock and Minerals:
hammer
chisel
hand-held magnifying lens
collection bag or old pillowcase
pencil and notebook

Butterflies:
net
holding envelopes
forceps
hand lens
collection bag or backpack
pencil and notebook

Tree Leaves:
sheets of paper
large book for holding pressed leaves

forceps
hand lens
collection bag or backpack
pencil and notebook

Bird Feathers:
forceps
holding envelopes
collection bag or backpack
hand lens
pencil and notebook

3. Collect numerous specimens.
4. Clean and fix your specimens. In the case of living animals, like butterflies, you will need to kill these specimens prior to preparation. The best way to kill butterflies is to leave them in their holding envelopes and put the envelope in a freezer. This method will preserve the butterfly without causing any wing damage.
5. Show your specimens in a suitable display case.
6. Label each specimen with its name and complete collection data.

Results If you are dedicated to your collection of specimens, you will soon accumulate a large holding of information. This wealth of information is the basis for the collection of specimens by scientists. Only through observation and investigation can advances be made in the life sciences.

Collections form a vital link in the scientific process. A collection can provide year's worth of valuable data with reference to time, age, and location. Additionally, a collection can serve as a comparative identification source. For example, if you have a bird feather that you are unable to properly identify, you could study other bird feather collections and determine the identity of your specimen.

Another important point about specimen collections is that they prevent confusion over the naming of newly discovered plants and animals. This potential confusion is avoided by requiring that each new scientific discovery be checked against all similar specimens in the world's collections. Only after this verification process has been completed is a newly discovered plant or animal officially named.

Further studies Many specimens are impractical for convenient collection. For example, the killing of butterflies can seriously harm the millions of rarer species. A better collection technique, in this case, is to use a camera as your collection equipment. Accurate photographs can be just as informative as actual specimens.

Make a specimen collection that consists exclusively of photographs. Remember to record all of the collection data for each photograph, just like you did with your "real" specimens. Clever display techniques can make photographs look visually "real." Can you mount your photographs in a realistic setting? Which specimen collection do you like better?

Did you know?

○ A dragon fly can fly up to 36 miles an hour for short distances.

○ As with many living species, butterflies come in a variety of sizes. Some, like New Guinea's Queen Alexandra's birdwing have a spectacular wingspan of almost 12 inches. Others, like a plain British moth, are tiny with spans of less than a tenth of an inch.

○ Most owls are night owls, or nocturnal. That means they hunt for food at night and sleep during the day.

Experiment 32

Why are fossils found in rock?

Materials   ❏ Safety goggles
❏ Work gloves
❏ Hard hat
❏ Hammer
❏ Chisel
❏ Small awl
❏ Brush
❏ Hand-held magnifying lens
❏ Toothbrush
❏ Water
❏ Collection bag or a pillowcase
❏ Pencil
❏ Notebook

Procedure

1. Read some basic books on rocks, minerals, and fossils. Ones you might try include: *Rocks, Minerals and Fossils of the World* by Chris Pellant; *A Field Guide to Rocks and Minerals* by Frederick H. Pough; *Rocks and Minerals* by R.F. Symes and the staff of the Natural History Museum, London; *Fossils: A Guide to Prehistoric Life* by Frank H.T. Rhodes, Herbert S. Zim, and Paul R. Shaffer; and *Rocks and Minerals: A Guide to Familiar Minerals, Gems, Ores and Rocks* by Herbert S. Zim and Paul R. Shaffer.

2. Visit, with an adult, a local limestone or other sedimentary rock deposit. This can be either a natural deposit or a rock dump site. Be sure to wear your hard hat.

   Sedimentary rocks include:

   Breccia
   Clay

Coal
Conglomerate
Flint
Limestone
Sandstone
Shale

3. Closely study the rocks for signs of fossils (FIG. 32-1). Following the instructions in your fossil collecting book, carefully split open a sedimentary rock. Be sure to wear your safety goggles and gloves when working with the chisel and hammer.
3. Use the magnifying lens to examine any potential fossil.
4. If the rock is a large one, cut around the fossil to remove the excess rock. Occasionally clean your work surface with the toothbrush and water.
5. Label the fossil with all of the available collection information: date, location of the rock, position of the rock.

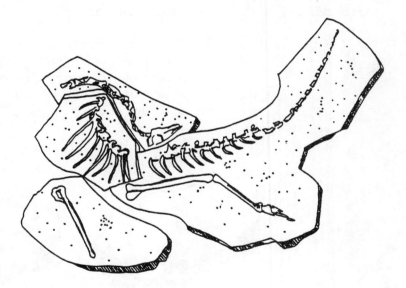

32-1 A fossil from a vertebrate

Results   *Fossils* are visual evidence of organisms that lived thousands of years ago. Fossils may be the organism's bark, shell, bone, or stem that has been replaced by the minerals from the surrounding water or soil. Other forms of fossils are the *casts*, or molds, of the dead plant or animal. In either case, a fossil is a rock replica of a dead organism.

One benefit that scientists derive from the study of fossils is an explanation of the evolution of life on earth. The science of studying

Why are fossils found in rock?   93

fossils is *paleontology* and the scientists who study fossils are called paleontologists.

The oldest fossils on record are *algae* with an age of one billion years. Fossils that old are difficult to find, however. The bulk of the fossil record is dated from 500 million years to the present day.

Further studies Sometimes it is impractical to remove a fossil from a rock. If this situation arises, you can make a plaster mold of the fossil. Here are the directions:

Materials
❒ Fossil
❒ Toothbrush
❒ Water
❒ Cardboard
❒ Petroleum jelly
❒ Plaster of paris

Procedure
1. Clear all loose rock, sand, and dust away from the fossil. (See FIG. 32-2.)
2. Enclose the fossil with cardboard as shown.
3. Coat the fossil with petroleum jelly to protect it from the plaster. Prepare the plaster of paris according to the directions on the package. Pour the plaster over the fossil. After the plaster has set, remove the cardboard ring and lift the plaster mold off the fossil.

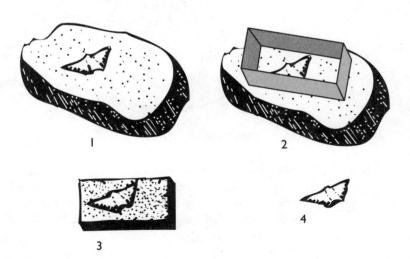

32-2 Making a simple plaster cast

4. Back in your home laboratory, you can make an accurate cast of this fossil. First, coat the inside of the mold with petroleum jelly so the cast will release from the mold. Then, make a batch of plaster of paris and pour it into the mold. When the plaster mixture has dried, remove the cast from the mold. You now have an accurate fossil replica. If you want, you can paint your cast.

Did you know?

○ A fossil forest was discovered in 1987 on Axel Heiberg Island, which is 700 miles from the North Pole.

○ Dinosaurs made significant evolutionary advances from 230 million years ago until 65 million years ago. This period in geology is called the Mesozoic Era—the Age of Dinosaurs.

Why is some water green?

Materials
☐ 2 gallons pond water
☐ 5-gallon aquarium
☐ Aerator pump
☐ Hand-held magnifying lens

Procedure
1. Collect 2 gallons of clear water from a local fresh-water pond.
2. Pour this water in a 5-gallon aquarium tank.
3. Insert the air hose from an aerator into the pond water.
4. Set the aquarium near a natural light source.

Results
After several weeks, the pond water will turn green. This green color will even be visible on the glass sides of the aquarium.

Simple green plants called algae are responsible for the green color. Algae functions just like plants that are found on land. They provide the aquatic community with oxygen and food products. Many algae are single-celled plants that float in the water or attach themselves to solid objects. Other forms of algae are found in colonies or as long, multi-celled filaments.

Freshwater algae can be divided into six general categories: blue-green algae, green algae, diatoms, stoneworts, euglenoids, and di-noflagellates. These last two algae groups also share single-celled animal characteristics. Based on the green color in your aquarium, your pond water sample contains predominately blue-green and green algae (See FIG. 33-1.) Some common forms of blue-green algae include Anabaena, Anacystis, Lyngbya, and Nostoc. Common green algae are Ankistrodesmus, Chlorella, Cladophora, Closterium, Spiro-gyra, and Volvox.

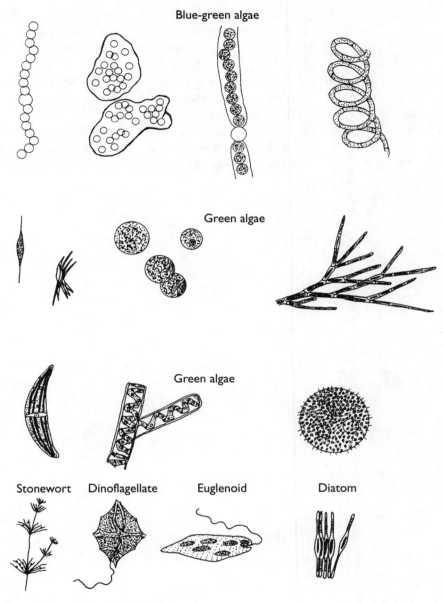

33-1 Types of freshwater algae

Further studies Return to the pond where you collected your original freshwater sample. Locate algae in this pond. Can you identify any of the algae? Are there any other types of algae present in the pond? Why didn't these algae types occur in your aquarium?

Large formations of blue-green algae can cause the water to stink. What does your pond smell like? Take a population survey of your pond. Is the algae able to support a large animal population?

○ *Carrageenan*, a gelatinous substance extracted from red algae, is used in ice cream and other frozen treats to prevent ice crystals from forming.

○ The green film you often see on fresh-water ponds is made up of duckweed, the smallest flowering plant in the world. Each plant is only one-thirtieth to one-fiftieth of an inch in diameter.

Part 6
The Young Physicist

Physics studies relationships in the material world by using mechanics, mathematics, and logic to arrive at solutions. These solutions try to answer two basic questions: Why does an event happen? How does an event occur?

The definition of physics comes from the Greek word "nature." In this case, nature means the composition of a thing. Therefore, physics is the understanding of the composition of a thing through the application of mechanics, mathematics, and logic.

Just as life sciences are a large grouping of several different scientific disciplines, physics encompasses many different disciplines. Physics deals with 10 disciplines: acoustics (see glossary), atomic structure, electricity, heat, magnetism, mechanics, nuclear energy, optics, radiation, and semiconductor technology.

Why does a telescope magnify objects?

Materials
- ❏ Two 8½-x-11-inch pieces of light cardboard or heavy paper
- ❏ Masking tape
- ❏ Scissors
- ❏ 4-x-12-inch piece of black velvet or heavy felt
- ❏ Nontoxic white glue
- ❏ 1½-inch-diameter convex lens 20 cm or less focal length
- ❏ 1-inch-diameter convex lens 5 cm.

Procedure
1. Roll one piece of the cardboard into a tight 8½-x-1-inch tube. Tape the tube together.
2. Roll the other piece of cardboard into a 8½-x-½-inch tube. Tape it together.
3. With the fabric, form a collar (or ring) around one end of the smaller tube; glue the collar in place. Slide the smaller tube inside the larger one. Does it fit loosely? If it does, add another layer or two of fabric to the collar. Glue the fabric in place. Keep adding layers until the tube fits snugly inside the larger one. You should still be able to slide the smaller tube in and out. (See FIG. 34-1.)
4. Gently press the 1-inch-diameter convex lens into the end of the smaller tube that is covered with the cloth.
5. Gently press the 1½-inch-diameter convex lens into either end of the larger tube.
6. Slide the cloth-covered end of the smaller tube into the end of the larger tube that is not holding the larger convex lens.
7. Focus your telescope by sliding the smaller tube in and out.

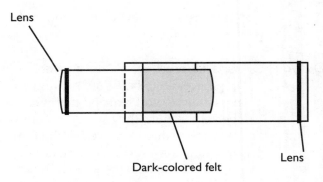

Lens

Lens

Dark-colored felt

34-1 Constructing a simple telescope

Results Your telescope will magnify distant objects. This type of telescope is called a Newtonian or Galilean telescope.

In this experiment, the larger lens is called the objective lens. It collects light from the object you are looking at and focuses the image as a bright image on the smaller lens.

The smaller lens is called the eyepiece. The eyepiece further magnifies the image.

This form of a telescope was first invented by Hans Lippershey in 1608. It wasn't until 1610, however, when *Galileo* built a telescope like Lippershey's that this method of object *magnification* became widely used. Figure 34-2 shows a refracting telescope and a reflecting telescope.

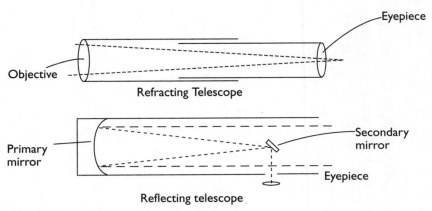

Eyepiece

Objective

Refracting Telescope

Primary mirror

Secondary mirror

Eyepiece

Reflecting telescope

34-2 Telescope types

Further studies In his experiments with telescopes, Galileo used a concave lens for the eyepiece. Try substituting this lens type for the convex one in your telescope. Does this substitution improve the image? Can you magnify distant objects to a higher degree with the concave eyepiece?

○ Hans Lippershey, a Dutch eyeglass maker, discovered the telescope accidentally. While making a pair of glasses, he held a lens in each hand and realized that when the lenses were lined up and peered through, they would magnify objects.

○ Although Galileo believed in the findings of Copernicus, who said that the Earth revolved around the sun, he was forced to renounce his beliefs. In Galileo's time, many people did not want to believe that the Earth was not the center of the universe. A famous legend has it that after Galileo made a public speech saying that the Earth stood still, he muttered under his breath: "But it *does* move."

Why does a microscope enlarge objects?

Materials   ❑ 8-inch piece of bare 22-gauge wire
❑ Nail
❑ Pliers

Procedure   1. Cut a piece of wire 8 inches long.

2. Bend one end of the wire around the nail. Twist the free end of the wire to the main body of the wire. This step should make a small loop in the wire. Remove the loop from the nail. Dip the wire loop in a cup of water. (See FIG. 35-1.) The water should fill the inside of the loop. Remove the water-filled loop from the water.
3. Looking through the water-filled loop, examine the type on this page.

Results   The water inside the loop forms a magnifying lens. Looking through it enlarges an object. This magnification is similar to the results obtained from a hand-held magnifying lens. A magnifying lens is the simplest form of a microscope.

   The standard laboratory compound microscope is more complex. In the compound microscope, there are a pair of lenses. (See FIG. 35-2.) Near the top of the microscope is an eyepiece lens. This lens is called the ocular.

   The average ocular has a magnification of 5X to 10X. This magnification is expressed as a multiplication of the image size, or power of magnification. Therefore, a 10X ocular will enlarge an object to 10 times its natural size.

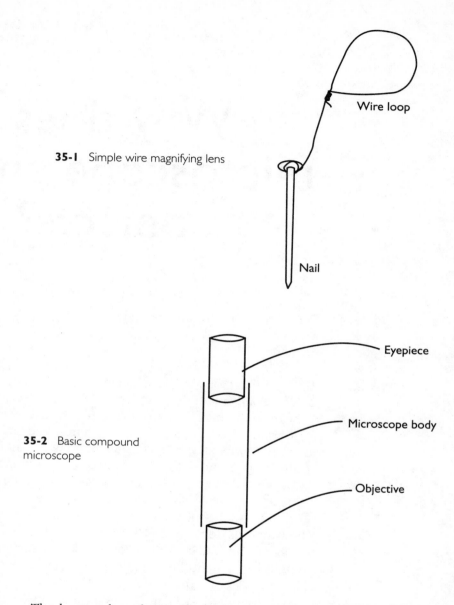

35-1 Simple wire magnifying lens

Wire loop

Nail

35-2 Basic compound microscope

Eyepiece

Microscope body

Objective

The lens at the other end of the microscope is the objective lens. The average objective has a magnification value of 10X to 60X. Most microscopes have several objectives each with a distinct magnification. These objectives are held in a revolving wheel called the nose-piece.

Further studies Based on the lens description of the compound microscope, try to build your own. Basically, you will need to construct an eyepiece

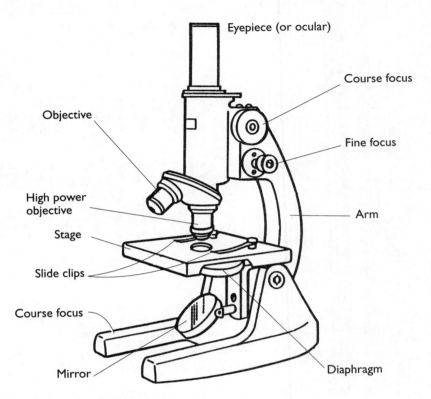

Eyepiece (or ocular)

Course focus

Objective

Fine focus

High power objective

Arm

Stage

Slide clips

Course focus

Mirror

Diaphragm

35-3 Parts of a microscope

and an objective. For each of these optic areas you will need a set of lenses.

Experiment with various lens combinations. Which lens combinations give you the best degree of magnification? Do moving your lenses increase the magnification? Does the resolution or clarity of the image decrease as the number of lenses increase? Try two plano-convex lenses for the eyepiece and two pairs of double-convex and plano-concave lenses for the objective. Does this improve the magnification of your compound microscope?

Did you know?
○ Although the principles behind the compound microscope were discovered by Zacharias Janssen in 1590, it was *Anton van Leeuwenhoek* who popularized the use of the microscope in science research.
○ The electron microscope uses electrons instead of light to magnify very small objects that can't be seen with the naked eye. An electron microscope is very powerful. It can make an object appear 200,000 times its actual size.

Why do submarines use periscopes?

Materials ❏ Four 8½-x-11-inch pieces of cardboard
❏ Two 3-inch square mirrors
❏ Masking tape

Procedure 1. Cut the four sheets of cardboard into the dimensions given in FIG. 36-1. Tape the pieces together as shown.
2. Make sure the rectangle is open at each end.
3. Carefully tilt one of the mirrors to a 45° angle and position it at one end of the rectangle.
4. Tape this mirror into position.
5. Carefully tilt and place the other square mirror into the opposite end of the cardboard tube. The two mirrors should be parallel and facing each other.
6. Tape this mirror into position.
7. Look through one of the openings.

Results By looking into one of the mirrors, you can see a reversed image. This image is produced by the other mirror. You can use this reversed-image ability to look around corners with your *periscope*.

Two characteristics are shared by every periscope. First, the two mirrors must be parallel with each other. This step is necessary to ensure the proper transmission of the image through the periscope tube.

The second characteristic of a periscope is that the mirrors must be positioned at a 45° angle. This angle is in reference to the axis of the periscope tube.

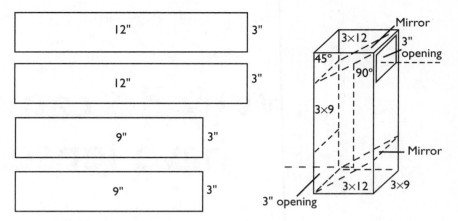

36-1 Constructing a periscope

The ability of periscopes to peer around corners has led to some interesting applications. For example, a submarine uses a periscope for viewing objects on the surface of the water while the submarine is submerged, or underwater.

Another form of the periscope is found in army tanks. These periscopes are actually giant prisms that allow the person inside the tank to view the outside terrain without leaving the tank or opening the protective hatch.

Finally, a periscope is useful for watching events such as the launch of a missile or rocket. With a periscope, observers are able to view the launch without being near the hot exhaust of the rocket's motors.

Further studies The periscope that you built is only 12 inches long. This limited length is impractical for many forms of viewing. Can you build a periscope that is longer than this model? What is the maximum length for a two-mirror periscope? Would the use of eyepiece lenses make the periscope's image sharper?

Did you know?
○ The first navigable submarine was built by Cornelius J. Drebbel of the Netherlands in 1620. The submarine was actually a rowboat covered with leather and operated by a dozen oarsmen underwater. Drebbel discovered that a substance called *saltpeter* could be used to keep the boat submerged for up to 15 hours.
○ Modern submarines use periscopes that are about 40 feet long when fully extended. These periscopes have tilting prisms that allow an observer to not only scan the horizon, but also the sky.

Why do cameras have lenses?

Materials
- ❑ Empty oatmeal box
- ❑ 2-inch square of aluminum foil
- ❑ Straight pin
- ❑ Scissors
- ❑ Masking tape
- ❑ Safety goggles
- ❑ Face mask
- ❑ Black spray paint
- ❑ Roll of Kodak 120 Panatomic-X film or any slow-speed (32 ASA or ISO value), black-and-white film

Procedure

1. Remove the lid from the empty oatmeal box.
2. Clean out all dust and leftover oatmeal.
3. With the scissors, carefully cut a 1-inch-square hole in the center of one side of the box. (See FIG. 37-1.) Use the scissors correctly. Remember, they are sharp and can cut you.
4. Wearing safety goggles and a face mask and working in a well-ventilated area, completely cover the inside and outside of the oatmeal box with the black spray paint. Ask an adult to help you with the paint. And be careful how you handle the can since it is pressurized and can hurt you if used incorrectly.
5. Be sure the aluminum foil is completely smooth. There must be no wrinkles in the surface of the foil.
6. Gently press the point of the straight pin through the center of the foil. Only the tip of the pin should pierce the foil. A properly made hole will be slightly larger than the diameter of a human hair.
7. When the paint has dried on the oatmeal box, tape the foil over the hole in the side of the oatmeal box. The pinhole in the foil should be in the exact center of the 1-inch-square hole.

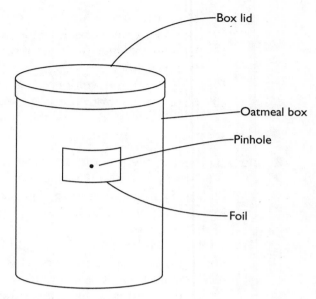

Box lid

Oatmeal box

Pinhole

Foil

37-1 Constructing a pinhole camera

8. Take the roll of film, your pinhole camera, and the masking tape inside a totally dark room or closet. Absolutely no light must enter.

9. Open the roll of film. Pull out the paper leader on the film. The film is taped to this leader. Find the beginning of the film. Carefully remove the beginning of the film from the paper leader. Measure out enough film to ring the inside of the oatmeal box. This ring of film should NOT cover the foil-covered opening in the side of the oatmeal box.

10. Tape this length of film to the inside of the oatmeal box. Again, be sure the film does NOT cover the foil opening in the side of the oatmeal box.

11. Roll up the remainder of the film and store it in a light-tight container.

12. Place the lid on the oatmeal box and tape the lid in place. This step is necessary to prevent stray light from striking the film inside the oatmeal box.

13. Cup your hand over the foil pinhole in the side of the oatmeal box.

14. Go outside into bright sunlight. Locate a suitable subject and set your camera on a solid surface.

15. Place your other free hand on the lid of the camera and your hand away from the foil pinhole.

16. Expose, or uncover, the foil for one minute.

17. When the time is up, cup your hand over the foil pinhole and take your camera back inside the dark room or closet.
18. Remove the film from your camera and place it inside a light-tight container.
19. Have the film developed.
20. Make a print from the processed negative and judge the *exposure*. Lengthen the exposure time if the print is too dark; shorten it if the print is too light.

Results Light enters the pinhole of your camera and strikes the film. The film is light sensitive and reacts to the presence of light. Even though the pinhole lacks a lens, it focuses the rays of light reflected from the subject of your photograph, and a picture forms on the film at the rear of the box.

But have you noticed the odd feature about your *negative?* The image on it is upside down. This effect is due to the straight-line movement of the subject's reflected light as it enters the pinhole.

In this example, light from the top of the subject moves in a straight downward path through the pinhole and finally lands on the lower portion of the negative. Likewise, the light reflected from the bottom portion of the subject travels to the upper area of the negative. Therefore, the negative is an inverted image of the subject.

Further studies One method for improving the quality of your photographs is to use a glass lens instead of a pinhole. A lens will increase the intensity of the light entering the oatmeal box. This brighter light will lead to a shorter exposure time. Additionally, a lens will enhance the resolution of the final image. But a problem exists with a direct substitution of a lens for the pinhole. Can you think of what this problem might be?

The problem is the *focal length* of the lens. Every lens has a focal length, or distance at which the transmitted image is sharp. The focal length determines the distance that the lens must be from the film. Try various lenses and lens combinations in your oatmeal box. Can you find any with the right focal length?

During these tests, don't waste your film. Place the lens or lens combination over the one-inch square-opening in the side of the oatmeal box. Point this opening at a bright light source. Now remove the lid from the oatmeal box and examine the inverted image on the box's rear wall. Use this technique until you find a lens with the right focal length. Your camera is now ready to make higher-quality photographs.

Did you know? ○ All cameras originate from a device used in ancient times called the *camera obscura*. Although no one knows exactly when the camera obscura was invented, there is a definite record of it being used in 350 B.C. The camera obscura consisted of a completely dark large room with a small opening on one outside wall. Some time in the first century A.D., a lens was used in place of the small opening.

○ The word "camera" comes from a Latin word meaning "enclosure" or "room."

Experiment 38

Why is light white?

Materials
- ❐ 3 spotlights
- ❐ Red glass or theater gel filter
- ❐ Blue glass or theater gel filter
- ❐ Green glass or theater gel filter
- ❐ White wall
- ❐ Masking tape

Procedure
1. Tape the red filter on the front of the spotlights.
2. Tape the blue filter to the front of another spotlight.
3. Tape the green filter to the front of the last spotlight.
4. Point all three lights at the white wall.
5. Turn on the red filter light. Observe the wall's color.
6. Turn on the blue filter light. Observe the wall's color.
7. Turn on the green filter light. Observe the wall's color.

Results The three *filters* are the *primary* colors for light. These primary colors are different from those for painting, which are red, yellow, and blue. When these primary paints are mixed together they form black.

Conversely, when the three primary colors of light are mixed together they make white. The combination of these three primary light colors is the reverse of splitting white light into its *visible spectrum*, or display of colors. Therefore, if you remove one of the primary-colored lights, the wall will no longer be white.

Further studies When all three of the primary lights are shining on the wall, the wall is white. Move your hand in front of the light and make a shadow on the wall. What color is your hand's shadow? Slowly move your hand along the wall. Does your shadow change colors?

Three distinct colors should form as shadows: yellow, magenta, and cyan. These are the *complementary* colors of light's primary colors. What primary combinations are needed to form these complementary colors? If this is the case of white light, why don't we make pretty colored shadows outside on a sunny day?

Did you know? ○ A rainbow is the spectrum formed opposite the sun by the *refraction* and reflection of the white light of the sun's rays through raindrops or mist. Rainbows are actually complete *concentric* circles, but you can only see the half of the circle above the horizon.

○ A rainbow's colors always appear in the same order: Red, orange, yellow, green, blue, indigo, and violet. You can remember the order by taking the first letter of each color and making a name: ROY G. BIV.

Experiment 39

Why does a compass needle point north?

Materials ❏ Magnet
❏ Large sewing needle
❏ Thread
❏ Drinking straw
❏ Two books of equal height
❏ Paper
❏ Pencil

Procedure 1. Hold the magnet in one hand and the needle in the other hand. The needle is sharp, be careful not to poke yourself or anyone else.

2. Rub the needle lengthwise along the south pole of the magnet. Repeat rubbing 30 times. Make sure that you always rub the needle in the same direction on the magnet. (To find the south pole, use a compass. The south pole of the bar magnet will attract the south pole of the compass.)

3. Put the magnet away.

4. Tie the thread around the center of the needle. When held by the thread, the needle should hang parallel to a tabletop.

5. Stand two books on their edges so that their tallest dimension is above the tabletop. (See FIG. 39-1.) Place the books about 6 inches apart.

6. Measure the height of your two books.

7. Cut the thread that is attached to the needle to a length that is slightly less than the height of the books.

8. Tie the other end of the thread around the center of the straw.

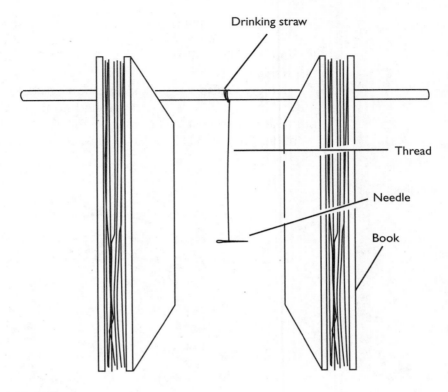

Drinking straw

Thread

Needle

Book

39-1 Simple compass

9. Place the straw between the two books. The needle should swing freely between the two books.
10. Position a piece of paper beneath the swinging needle. Can you label the four main compass points (north, south, east, and west) by watching this swinging needle?

Results Your needle is a simple compass. As it swings on the thread, the magnetized needle is pointing toward the magnetic north and south poles of the earth.

When the needle is rubbed along the magnet, the needle becomes magnetized. In this condition, the needle will align itself with the fields of magnetism that circle the earth. These fields begin at the North and South Poles. Therefore, the needle always points to the north and south. This fact is true for all compasses.

Early sailing countries were the first to make use of this phenomenon. In 1100, the Chinese floated small magnetized pieces of iron in a bowl of water. This moving needle acted as a primitive compass. By the 1300s, more complex compasses were being used in sailing vessels, making possible accurate ocean navigation.

Further studies In its present condition, your simple compass isn't very helpful. Only two directions, north and south, are indicated. How would you modify your needle compass so that is would indicate all four compass positions?

Could you also use the modification to label 32 different compass points? In other words, could you find north, north by east, north by northeast, northeast by north, northeast, and northeast by east. Identifying these 32 compass points is called boxing the compass. (See FIG. 39-2.)

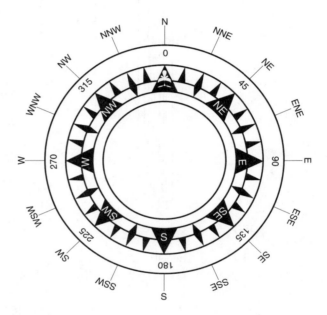

39-2 Compass card (rose)

Did you know?
- There are two compass "norths." True north is the direction on a map indicating the geographic North Pole. Magnetic north is the compass indication for the magnetic North Pole.
- In his voyages, Christopher Columbus used a compass and a method of navigation called *dead reckoning*. Dead reckoning estimates the position of a boat from charts of courses that other boats have used, along with a determination of distance covered and the effect of drift. In Columbus's day, sailors also used celestial navigation, which determines position from the fixed position of the stars. Columbus, however, rarely used this method, relying almost solely on the compass.

Experiment 40

Why do magnets attract?

Materials
- ❏ Compass
- ❏ 8-inch iron rod with ⅜-inch rebar (re-enforcement)
- ❏ Work gloves
- ❏ Hammer
- ❏ Ten paper clips

Procedure

1. Position the compass on a flat old tabletop or workbench.
2. Study the direction of north and south.
3. Wearing the work gloves and wrapping a towel around the bar, place one hand around the middle of the iron rod.
4. Move the iron rod so that one end is pointing north and the other end is pointing south. Do not let the rod touch the table.
5. Position the rod so that the end that is pointing north touches the tabletop.
6. Grasp the hammer in your free hand. Ask an adult to help you with the next step.
7. Strike the south end of the iron rod once firmly with the hammer. Be sure to strike the bar sharply, if you hit it too gently, the experiment won't work. Be careful not to miss and strike your fingers.
8. Touch one end of the iron rod to a pile of paper clips. (See FIG. 40-1.)

Results Your iron rod has become a magnet and will pick up the paper clips. When the hammer hit the iron rod, all of the molecules moved slightly and realigned themselves according to the magnetic field of the north and south poles. Therefore, the iron rod became a magnet.
You can further prove this theory of molecular movement pro-

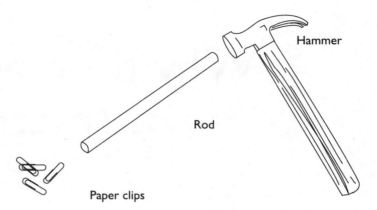

40-1 Magnetizing an iron rod

ducing magnetism by cutting the iron rod in half. Both halves of the iron rod will be equally magnetized.

Further studies
Another experiment to test molecular movement and magnetism involves heating the iron rod. Be sure to have an adult work with you on this experiment. You'll need several hot pads and you must be very careful. The rod will be extremely hot!

Have an adult place the magnetized iron rod inside an oven set for high heat (over 500° F). Leave the iron rod in the oven long enough for it to become completely heated, about 15 minutes. An adult, who is using hot pads, should very carefully remove the hot iron rod. The adult should place the rod on two hot pads and let it cool. Do *not* touch the hot rod.

There should be no magnetic source near the iron rod as it cools. Once the iron rod has cooled, place it near the paper clips. What happened to the paper clips? Is the iron rod still magnetized? How does this heating experiment prove the molecular movement theory of magnetism?

Did you know?
○ All objects made of iron are magnetic. The Eiffel Tower in Paris, France is made entirely of steel, which is strengthened iron.
○ Magnets occur naturally in the ground. Lodestone is a magnetic stone made from iron ore. Thousands of years ago, the Chinese studied the magnetic properties of lodestone.

Why does a dropped book fall?

Materials ❏ Book

Procedure 1. Hold the book several inches above a tabletop.
2. Drop the book.

Results The dropped book hit the tabletop. The influence of gravity caused the book to fall instead of rising and hitting the ceiling.

Gravitation, or the attraction between two masses, is one physical science that remains largely unexplained. Researchers know that gravity holds the universe together by keeping moons, planets, and stars in orbit. And numerous other examples prove that gravity exists, but the real cause of gravity is still somewhat of a mystery.

The closest attempt at defining gravity came from *Albert Einstein*, who theorized in 1929 that gravitational attraction and *electromagnetism* might be related. Even Isaac Newton in his 1687 publication of the laws of gravitation ignored the question of cause.

Further studies

In this experiment, you will do a "trick" that will appear to defy gravity. Actually, the "trick" is an optical illusion. Here's what you'll need for the trick: two matching table forks, a cork, a nail, and a drinking glass.
1. Stick the forks into the cork. Both forks should be on opposite sides of the cork and near its fatter end (FIG. 41-1). This is the most critical part of making this trick work.

2. Insert nail into the center of the cork's smaller end (FIG. 41-2).
3. Position the free end of the nail on the lip of the drinking glass
   (FIG. 41-3). Carefully move the nail around until the cork and forks
   balance (FIG. 41-3).

   Is this trick really defying gravity? Why don't the forks fall? What
is the secret behind this illusion?

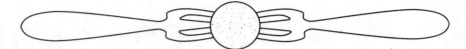

41-1 Inserting the forks into the cork

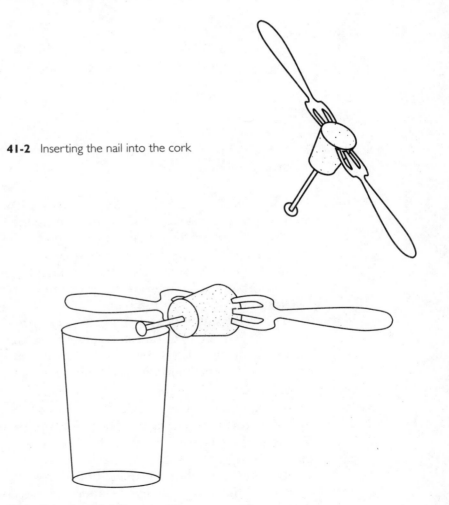

41-2 Inserting the nail into the cork

41-3 Balancing the forks

Did you know?
- Most of us have learned that Sir Issac Newton discovered gravity when he noticed an apple fall from a tree on his family farm. Actually, he had been studying gravity before this occurrence. The French writer Voltaire popularized the story of the apple.
- After publishing his theory of gravity, Newton did little scientific work. He became a politician and was made director of the mint in England instead.

Experiment 42

Why does hot air rise?

Materials
- ❏ Large heat-resistant bowl
- ❏ Empty plastic soda bottle
- ❏ Balloon
- ❏ Rubber band
- ❏ Ice water
- ❏ Hot water

Procedure

1. Fill the large bowl with ice water.
2. Stand the empty bottle in the ice water. Don't let any of the ice water enter the bottle.
3. After 5 minutes, place the balloon over the top of the bottle. Secure the balloon with the rubber band.
4. Remove the bottle from the ice water and set it on the tabletop.
5. Empty the ice water from the large bowl.
6. Fill the large bowl with boiling water.
7. Place the bottle in the hot water. (See FIG. 42-1.)

Results Expanding air inside the bottle caused the balloon to inflate. The air inside the bottle was first cooled by the ice water. This air was trapped inside the bottle by the balloon. The air was then heated by the hot water. As it heated, the air expanded—or took up more space—and entered the balloon. Expanding air becomes lighter and rises. This principle is the same one that powers hot-air balloons.

Further studies To learn more about the expansion and contraction of air, try the following: Carefully pour boiling water into the plastic bottle to a depth of 3 inches. Swirl the water around the inside of the bottle for 30 seconds. Pour the water out. Immediately cap the bottle and place it in a freezer.

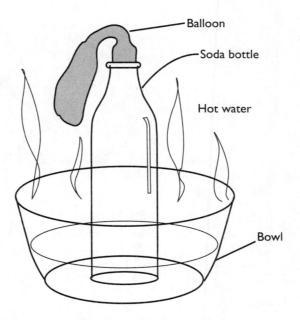

Balloon

Soda bottle

Hot water

Bowl

42-1 Testing the principle of a hot-air balloon

What happened to the bottle? Did it remain the same? How did it change?

Try the experiment again. What happened to the bottle this time?

How much your bottle changes will depend on several things: How tightly you capped the bottle. How cold your freezer is. And how long it took you to cap the bottle.

In this experiment, you saw two things happen. In the first part, you saw how air, a gas, expands when it's heated. In the second part, you saw how it contracts when it's chilled.

Did you know?

○ In 1783, two French brothers, *Jacques Etienne* and *Joseph Michel Montgolfier*, flew the first hot-air balloon. Their first flight was unmanned and climbed to an altitude of 35 feet. Within, one year of this flight, the Montgolfiers flew a seven-passenger balloon to an altitude of 3,000 feet. (See FIG. 42-2.)

○ Areas of heated air in the atmosphere are called *low-pressure* areas. When this heated air rises above the surrounding air, it creates a *thermal air current*. Birds and hang gliders often circle in thermal air currents so that they will be lifted higher into the sky.

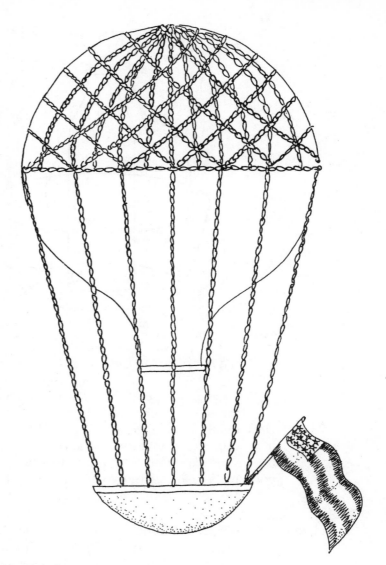

42-2 Hot-air balloon

Suppliers & Services

Suppliers   CAROLINA BIOLOGICAL SUPPLY COMPANY
Burlington, NC 27215
(919) 584-0381

The leading supplier of scientific materials for schools and other education institutions is Carolina Biological Supply Company. Living, as well as preserved, specimens can be purchased from the company. It also offers an excellent selection of scientific equipment for research in every scientific discipline.

CHILDCRAFT EDUCATION CORPORATION
20 Kilmer Road
Edison, NJ 08818
(809) 631-5657

Educational toys and other goodies fill the pages of Childcraft's 47-page color catalog. Among the many items of educational merit are several of scientific interest. Most of the products sold by Childcraft Education Corporation are for youngsters under 13 years of age.

EDMUND SCIENTIFIC COMPANY
101 E. Gloucester Pike
Barrington, NJ 08007

Edmund Scientific Company started as a scientific surplus equipment dealer. This business quickly mushroomed into a general-purpose science "thing" dealer. You can purchase virtually any exotic scientific tool that you will ever need or want from this company. From lasers to giant 8-inch reflecting telescopes, Edmund Scientific Company has it all.

GULF COAST RESEARCH LABORATORY
P.O. Box AG
Ocean Springs, MS 39564

Gulf Coast Research Laboratory is an educational institution that prints a marvelous set of educational leaflets. Each of these leaflets discusses a separate marine biology topic. The information is accurate and free of charge (check with the firm for a change in this policy).

HEATH COMPANY
Benton Harbor, MI 49022

Heath Company's chief claim to fame is its offering of high-quality electronic construction kits. These are the finest kits that you will find anywhere on the market. These kits range from easy-to-construct radio projects to complex digital computers. Each kit comes complete with all of the parts necessary to build a project. Additionally, a detailed set of assembly instructions will guide you through the construction process.

JDR MICRODEVICES
1224 S. Bascom Avenue
San Jose, CA 95128
(800) 538-5000

JDR Microdevices is an electronics parts supplier. It's prices are reasonable and its service is prompt. If you have any trouble locating the parts needed for any of the electronics experiments in this book, call JDR Microdevices.

RADIO SHACK (Local stores)

Many of the electronic parts needed for the experiments in this book have been referenced with Radio Shack catalog numbers. You should be able to find most of the parts in your local store. But if Radio Shack is out of a particular part, you can order it. An average order will arrive in less than one week.

Services NATIONAL AUDUBON SOCIETY
950 Third Avenue
New York, NY 10022

NATIONAL WILDLIFE FEDERATION
1412 16th Street, N.W.
Washington, D.C. 20036

WORLD WILDLIFE FUND
1255 23rd Street, N.W.
Washington, D.C. 20037

AUDUBON ZOOLOGICAL GARDEN
6500 Magazine Street
New Orleans, LA 70118

CENTRAL PARK ZOO
5th Avenue and 64th Street
New York, NY 10021

LINCOLN PARK ZOOLOGICAL GARDENS
Stockton Drive at Fullerton Avenue
Chicago, IL 60614

LOS ANGELES ZOO
5333 Zoo Drive
Los Angeles, CA 90027

NATIONAL ZOO
National Zoological Park
Washington, D.C. 20560

ART, SCIENCE & TECHNOLOGY INSTITUTE
Dupont Circle Metro 2018 R Street, N.W.
Washington, D.C. 20009

ASTRONOMY PROGRAM
University of Maryland
College Park, MD 20742

DEPARTMENT OF ENTOMOLOGY
New Mexico State University
Las Cruces, NM 88003

FLORIDA STATE COLLECTION OF ARTHROPODS
Division of Plant Industry
P.O. Box 1269
Gainesville, FL 32602

GODDARD INSTITUTE FOR SPACE STUDIES
2880 Broadway
New York, NY 10025

JET PROPULSION LABORATORY
4800 Oak Grove Drive
Pasadena, CA 91109

NATIONAL SPACE SCIENCE DATA CENTER
Goddard Flight Center
Greenbelt, MD 20771

NEW YORK PUBLIC LIBRARY
5th Avenue and 42nd Street
New York, NY 10018

PHILADELPHIA ACADEMY OF NATURAL SCIENCES
19th Street and Benjamin Franklin Parkway
Philadelphia, PA 19102

Smithsonian National Museums

SMITHSONIAN INSTITUTION BUILDING
ANACOSTIA MUSEUM
ARTHUR M. SACKLER GALLERY
ARTS AND INDUSTRIES BUILDING
ENID A. HAUPT GARDEN
FRER GALLERY OF ART
HIRSHHORN MUSEUM AND SCULPTURE GARDEN
INTERNATIONAL GALLERY
NATIONAL AIR AND SPACE MUSEUM
NATIONAL MUSEUM OF AFRICAN ART
NATIONAL MUSEUM OF AMERICAN ART
NATIONAL MUSEUM OF AMERICAN HISTORY
NATIONAL MUSEUM OF NATURAL HISTORY
NATIONAL PORTRAIT GALLERY
NATIONAL ZOOLOGICAL PARK
RENWICK GALLERY
NATIONAL GALLERY OF ART
Washington, D.C. 20560

U.S. PATENT AND TRADEMARK OFFICES
Washington, D.C. 20231

U.S. GEOLOGICAL SURVEY NATIONAL CENTER
Reston, VA 22092

Glossary

absorbency   The capacity to absorb or take up.

acid   A compound that reacts with a base to form a salt and is capable of turning blue litmus paper red.

acoustics   Relating to science of sound dealing with its production, transmission, and reception.

aerobatic   An aerial maneuver performed by an aircraft.

aerodynamics   The science dealing with air motions and its effect on airborne bodies.

ailerons   An aircraft's control surface that governs roll.

airfoil   A design structure that generates a desired motion effect when it is introduced into an air flow. Airfoils can be found on wings, as well as aircraft propellers.

algae   Any of a group of single-celled aquatic plants.

alkalie   Another term for a base.

architect   A person who designs and writes plans for houses and other buildings.

artificially   Done by humans, not nature.

astronomy   A science that studies the movements, compositions, and influences of celestial bodies atomic structure—the representation of a chemical element in terms of the number of protons in its nucleus along with any orbiting electrons.

atmosphere   The air surrounding earth.

atmospheric data   Information about the air around earth.

axis   The invisible straight line that the earth rotates around.

barometric pressure   The pressure of the atmosphere.

base   A compound that reacts with an acid to form a salt and will turn red litmus paper blue.

biochemistry   A science that studies the chemical compounds and processes that happen in organisms.

biology   A science that studies the processes of organisms.

biplanes   Two-winged aircraft.

blueprint   A detailed plan for making something. Also, a blueprint is a photosensitive process that produces a blue image on a white background. An uncommon variation of the blueprint is to print a white image on a blue background. Blueprints are used by engineers and architects for producing working prints.

botany A science that studies the structure and processes of plants.

Brequet, Louis and Jacques French aviation pioneer brothers who flew the first helicopter in 1907.

buoyancy The ability of an object to rise when put in a liquid.

buttress—a stone, masonry, or wood structure that supports a wall or a building.

canopy The fabric part of the parachute that catches the air.

capillary action An adhesion attraction between a solid and a liquid that results in the liquids rise or fall.

carrageenan A red algae. Extracts of the algae are used in foods such as ice cream.

cast An impression in plaster, sand, or other material.

chemistry The science of studying the structure, reactions, and properties of elements, molecules, ions, and compounds.

chlorophyll A photosynthetic compound found in the plant chloroplasts.

chloroplast A plant structure that contains chlorophyll and contributes to the production of starch.

cirrus White, feathery clouds.

comets An orbiting celestial body with a bright center and a variously elongated tail.

complementary Two contrasting colors that when combined form a neutral color.

compress To squeeze a liquid or gas into a reduced volume.

concave lens A lens that is rounded inward.

concavo-convex One side of a lens curves inward; the other side curves outward.

concentric Circles with a common center.

condensation The act of changing from a gas or vapor to a liquid.

condense To reduce matter into a denser form.

consume To eat, drink, or use up.

convex lens A lens that is rounded outward.

convexo-concave One side of a lens curves outward; the other side curves inward.

cortex The bark or outer layer.

culture Food for growing bacteria and molds.

cumulus White, dense clouds seen in good weather.

dead reckoning An estimate of a ship's position from charts of courses that other boats have used, along with a determination of distance covered and the effect of drift.

da Vinci, Leonardo An Italian painter and engineer from 1452–1519.

Darwin, Charles An English naturalist from 1809–1882.

descent The act of going from a higher place to a lower one.

dew Tiny droplets of water that form when cool nights follow warm days.

dew point The temperature when water vapor begins to condense.

Doppler effect A change in wave frequency that increases or decreases with relation to the speed and distance between the wave's source and its destination.

double-concave Both surfaces of a lens curve inward.

double-convex Both surfaces of a lens curve outward.

drag A force limiting the movement of an aircraft through the air.

eclipse The total or partial obscuring of one celestial object by another one.

ecology The study of the interrelationship between organisms and their environment.

Edison, Thomas A. An American inventor who lived from 1847–1931.

Einstein, Albert A German physicist from 1879–1955.

electrode A material made into a conductor for forming an electrical contact.

electrolyte A nonmetallic material made into a conductor through ionic movement.

electron A small negatively charged particle.

electromagnetism Magnetism generated by electrical current.

elevators A moveable airfoil on the tail of an airplane for moving the airplane up and down.

erosion To diminish or destroy a substance through a slow and methodical application of a reducing agent.

evaporate To turn from a liquid to a vapor or gas.

exposure The act of uncovering something. In photography, the length of time light is allowed to reach the film.

Faraday, Michael The English chemist living from 1791–1867.

fertilize To make productive.

fiber A very thin thread and the material made from thread.

filter A material such as a piece of glass that modifies the color of light passing through it.

focal length The distance from a lens at which the image is clear.

forecast To predict, or say, what is going to happen.

fossil An organism or other organic matter preserved in a mineralized or petrified condition.

Galileo An Italian astronomer from 1564-1642. Galileo's real name was Galilei.

genetics A science that studies the developmental variation and heredity of an organism.

geotropism A growth factor in plants that is effected by gravity.

germinate To start to grow or sprout.

glycerine A colorless, odorless liquid.

gnomon A shadow indicator on a sundial.

gravitation The force that pulls two objects together.

gravity The pull of the earth, near its surface, that gives an object weight.

gully A ditch made by running water.

helium A light, colorless, nonflammable gas.

humidity Moisture in the atmosphere.

hydroponic gardening Growing plants in nutrient solutions without soil.

hyphae long, thin threads on mlds.

ion An atom with an electrical charge.

ionization The partial or total conversion of matter into ions.

keystone The wedge-shaped piece at the top of an arch. The keystone is used to keep that arch from collapsing.

knot A measurement of a ship's speed in nautical miles per hour.

latitude A distance measured in degrees. Measurement is north or south from the equator to the poles.

Leeuwenhoek, Anton A Dutch naturalist from 1632–1723.

lift A force on an airfoil that raises the aircraft up and counteracts the force of gravity.

litmus paper A paper that has been treated with litmus. Litmus is a coloring material that is derived from lichens. Blue litmus paper turns red in acids, and red litmus turns blue in alkaline solutions.

low-pressure Areas of heated air in the atmosphere.

magnification An enlargement factor.

Maxwell, James C. A Scottish physicist from 1831–1879.

Mendel, Gregor Johann The Austrian botanist born in 1822.

mercury A heavy, silvery, liquid metal used in thermometers and barometers.

meteorology The science of weather and weather forecasting.

microbiology The science of microorganisms.

molecular Produced or caused by molecules.

molecule Atoms joined together in a certain structure.

Montgolfier, J. E. and J. M. The French ballooning brothers born in the mid 1700s.

negative A photographic image in which the light and dark areas are reversed.

neutral A liquid that is neither an acid nor a base.

Newton, Sir Isaac An English mathematician from 1642–1727.

nimbus Low shapeless clouds that produce snow or rain.

nutrient Nourishment or food.

orbit The path the moon follows around the earth.

oxidation A process of combining a compound with oxygen.

paleontology A science that studies fossils and prehistoric environments.

periscope An instrument with mirrors that lets you see over or around things.

perspiration The process of sweating.

phase A stage in the moon's trip around earth.

pH A representation of the hydrogen-ion concentration that indicates acidity and alkalinity in terms of a negative logarithm.

photosynthesis The production of carbohydrates through chlorophyll reacting with light energy.

phototropism A growth factor in plants that is affected by light.

physiology A science that studies the functions of organisms.

pitch An aircraft's up and down movement as controlled by the horizontal stabilizer.

plano-concave One side of a lens curves inward; the other side is flat.

plano-convex One side of a lens curves outward; the other side is flat.

pollen A fine powder made by plants.

pollination The act of carrying pollen from one flower to another.

precipitates To separate from a solution and to fall out.

precipitation The depositing of rain or snow on the earth.

prediction The act of saying what might happen in the future.

primary The basic or most elementary part.

psychrometer A device with two thermometers (one wet and one dry) that indicates the relative humidity of the atmosphere.

Ramsay, William A British chemist from 1852–1916.
reflection The mirror or production of light or sound waves from a surface.
relative humidity The ratio of the amount of water vapor in the atmosphere to the amount of vapor that the atmosphere can hold.
refraction The bending of light rays as they pass through the earth's atmosphere.
respiration The processes of supplying oxygen to an organism's cells.
rhizoid A rootlike structure through which a mold obtains food.
rudder A moveable airfoil at the back of an airplane for controlling direction.

saltpeter Sodium nitrate and potassium nitrate.
saturate To fill completely so that an object cannot hold more. For example, a cloth or sponge can become so full of water that it cannot soak up any more.
sedimentary rock Rock formed by chemical and physical actions on organic sediment.
skewback The structure that faces the voussoirs of an arch.
spectrum An array or series of wavelengths. These could be light, sound, energy waves.
sporangium The case in which the spores of a mold are formed.
springer The stone that is at the base of an arch.
stolon A surface root of a mold.
supersaturated solution A solution that contains more material than it is normally capable of holding.
surface tension The attractive force that draws molecules together on the surface of a liquid.

template A pattern that is used as a guide for making or cutting something.
thermal air current Heated air that has risen above the surrounding air.
thrust A force the reacts against drag and moves a body forward like an aircraft.
Torricelli, Evangelista An Italian mathematician from 1608–1647.

visible Able to be seen.
voussoir The wedge-shaped pieces forming the body of an arch.

waning moon A moon that is reducing in size and intensity.

waxing moon A moon the is increasing in size and intensity.

Wright, Orville and Wilbur The American aviation pioneer brothers born in the late 1800s.

yaw Movement about a vertical axis (left to right) in an aircraft.

zoology A science that studies animals.

Bibliography

Aldrich, Arthur. *Flowers and Flowering Plants*. New York: Franklin
  Watts, 1976.

Berger, Melvin. *Lights, Lenses and Lasers*. New York: G.P. Putnam's
  Sons, 1987.

Brown, Robert J. *200 Illustrated Science Projects for Children*. Blue
  Ridge Summit: TAB Books, 1987.

———. *333 Science Tricks & Experiments*. Blue Ridge Summit: TAB
  Books, 1984.

Brown, Vinson. *How to Make a Nature Museum*. Boston: Little,
  Brown and Company, 1954.

Burt, William Henry, and Richard Philip Grossenheider. *A Field
  Guide to the Mammals*. Boston: Houghton Mifflin Company,
  1964.

Cole, Gerald A. *Textbook of Limnology*. Saint Louis: The C .V.
  Mosby Company, 1975.

Diamonstein, Barbaralee. *American Architecture Now II*. New York:
  Rizzoli International Publications, Inc., 1985.

Dowden, Anne Ophelia. *From Flower to Fruit*. New York: Thomas
  Y. Crowell, 1984.

Eddy, Samuel, and A. C. Hodson. *Taxonomic Keys to the Common
  Animals of the North Central States*. Minneapolis: Burgess
  Publishing Company, 1961.

Engle, Eloise. *Parachutes: How They Work*. New York: G.P.
  Putnam's Sons, 1972.

Freeman, Mae, and Ira Freeman. *Fun with Science*. New York:
  Random House, 1943.

Guise, David. *Design and Technology in Architecture*. New York:
  John Wiley & Sons, Inc., 1985.

Huntington, Roger. *Thompson Trophy Racers*. Osceola: Motorbooks
  International, 1989.

Jones, Lloyd S. *U. S. Fighters*. Blue Ridge Summit: Aero Books,
  1975.

Keen, Martin L. *The How and Why Wonder Science Book of Science Experiments*. New York: Wonder Books, 1962.

Klots, Alexander B. *A Field Guide to the Butterflies*. Boston: Houghton Mifflin Company, 1951.

Knott, J., and Dave Prochnow. *101 Projects, Plans, and Ideas for the High-Tech Household*. Blue Ridge Summit: TAB Books, 1986.

Kjellstrom, Bjorn. *Be an Expert with Map & Compass*. New York: Charles Scribner's Sons, 1975.

Lambert, David, and the Diagram Group. *The Dinosaur Data Book*. New York: Avon Books, 1990.

Lanners, Edi. *Secrets of 123 Classic Science Tricks and Experiments*. Blue Ridge Summit: TAB Books, 1987.

Lillie, David W. *Our Radiant World*. Blue Ridge Summit: TAB Books, 1987.

Lutz, Frank E., Paul S. Welch, Paul S. Galtsoff, and James G. Needham. *Culture Methods for Invertebrate Animals*, reprint. New York: Dover Publications, Inc., 1959.

Needham, James G., and Paul R. Needham. *A Guide to the Study Freshwater Biology*. San Francisco: Holden-Day, Inc., 1962.

Newhall, Beaumont. *The History of Photography*. New York: The Museum of Modern Art, 1964.

Nuttgens, Patrick. *The Pocket Guide to Architecture*. New York: Simon and Schuster, 1980.

Oldroyd, Harold. *The Natural History of Flies*. New York: W W Norton & Company, Inc., 1964.

Pabian, Roger K. *Record in Rock*. Lincoln: University of Nebraska Conservation and Survey Division, 1970.

Peterson, Roger Tory, and Margaret McKenny. *A Field Guide to Wildflowers of Northeastern and Northcentral North America*. Boston: Houghton Mifflin Company, 1968.

Petrides, George A. *A Field Guide to Trees and Shrubs of Northeastern and Central North America*. Boston: Houghton Mifflin Company, 1973.

Pfeiffer, Bruce Brooks, and Gerald Nordland. *Frank Lloyd Wright: In the Realm of Ideas*. Carbondale: Southern Illinois University Press, 1988.

Pough, Frederick H. *A Field Guide to Rocks and Minerals*. Boston: Houghton Mifflin Company, 1976.

Prochnow, Dave. *Chip Talk: Projects in Speech Synthesis*, Blue Ridge Summit: TAB Books, Inc., 1987.

————. *Superconductivity: Experiments in a New Technology*. Blue Ridge Summit: TAB Books, 1989.

Rhoads, Frank H.T., Herbert S. Zim, and Paul R. Shaffer. *Fossils: A Guide to Prehistoric Life*. New York: Golden Press, 1962.

Ruggiero, Michael, Alan Mitchell, and Philip Burton. *Spotter's Handbook*. New York: Mayflower Books, 1979.

Salvadori, Mario. *Why Buildings Stand Up: The Strength of Architecture*. New York: W W Norton & Company, Inc., 1980.

Sootin, Harry. *Light Experiments*. New York: W W Norton & Company, Inc., 1963.

———. *Science Experiments with Sound*. New York: W W Norton & Company, Inc., 1964.

Symes, Dr. R.F., and the staff of the Natural History Museum, London. *Rocks and Minerals*. New York: Alfred A. Knopf, 1988.

Walpole, Brenda. *Fun with Science: Light*. New York: Warwick Press, 1987.

Wells, Susan, Robert M. Pyle, and N. Mark Collins. *The ICUN Invertebrate Red Data Book*. Gland: IUCN, 1983.

Wood, Robert. *Physics for Kids*. Blue Ridge Summit: TAB, 1990.

Zim, Herbert S., PhD. and Alexander C. Martin, PhD. *Flowers: A Guide to Familiar American Wildflowers*. New York: Golden Press, 1991.

———. *Trees: A Guide to Familiar American Trees*. New York: Golden Press, 1991.

———. Paul R. Shaffer. *Rocks and Minerals: A Guide to Familiar Minerals, Gems, Ores and Rocks*. New York: Golden Press, 1964.

Index